Royal Palaces
of Europe

Royal Palaces of Europe

HUGH MONTGOMERY-MASSINGBERD

CHARTWELL
BOOKS, INC.

FOR JUDY

Published by
CHARTWELL BOOKS, INC.
A Division of BOOK SALES, INC.
110 Enterprise Avenue
Secaucus, New Jersey 07094

This book was designed and produced by
John Calmann and Cooper Ltd, London

© 1983 John Calmann and Cooper Ltd

ISBN 0–89009–794–1

Filmset in Great Britain by Keyspools Ltd, Golborne
Printed in Italy by Canale SpA

Contents

Introduction

'The palaces of kings', wrote Tom Paine, 'are built on the ruins of the bowers of paradise.' To this disgruntled tax collector and his revolutionary disciples in the late eighteenth century the concept of a royal palace, with its ceremonial and court life, was the unacceptable expression of absolute monarchy. Versailles, the quintessential royal palace so slavishly imitated all over Europe in the eighteenth century, was the prime target of the mob in the French Revolution.

Like so many royal palaces, Versailles began life as a hunting-lodge, recalling an earlier pattern of monarchy which depended upon how long the food supplies of the neighbourhood held out. Medieval monarchs tended to move from place to place as politics and the appetite of the court required. For practical reasons the residences of kings were not so much palaces as fortresses; the round tower at Amboise, for instance, recalls medieval warfare. By the end of the fifteenth century, however, the use of artillery on one level and, on a higher plane, the spread of the Italian Renaissance, had made the medieval fortified castle obsolete.

After his accession to the throne of France in 1515, François I built the Renaissance wing at Blois with its spiral staircase and the enormous 'hunting-box' of Chambord with its ordered arrangement of rooms (quite unlike the interior of a medieval castle). In Paris, the king's architect Pierre Lescot gave the Louvre (later to become the biggest royal palace in the world) its specifically French Renaissance character. Finally at another old hunting-lodge, the French 'Mannerist' version of the Renaissance reached its apogee with an interior splendidly decorated by the Italian School of Fontainebleau. A significant step in the development of the idea of the 'royal palace' was the King's gallery at Fontainebleau – the first of its kind.

In Germany, where the Renaissance came a little later, the Munich Residenz was built in the middle of a city arranged around half-a-dozen courtyards. In Denmark, the royal palace of Frederiksborg expressed an emphatically northern version of the Renaissance with its asymmetrical towers. In England, where acceptance of the Renaissance was held up by the Reformation, the Tudor Hampton Court stands as the best example of a royal palace from this period, though it was originally built for a commoner. The first truly classical building here, Inigo Jones's Palladian Banqueting House in Whitehall, was not completed until a century later.

The Alhambra in Spain, built from 1526 for Charles V, has been described as the most 'classic' palace in Europe, with its round courtyard modelled on Hadrian's villa. The Escorial was more in the style of a Spanish feudal castle. Philip II's monastic way of life in this vast convent-palace personified the union of State and Church while the Escorial's austere architecture hinted at the beginnings of the Early Baroque.

The familiar closed courtyards of the Renaissance palaces were now to be replaced in the exuberant age of the Baroque by the open *cour d'honneur*. The Italian ideal of a villa set on an axial approach with a park beyond was developed at Versailles into a symbolic network of rays radiating around *Le Roi Soleil*. Inside, elaborate enfilades of state apartments, all with their own ceremonial purpose, completed the courtly ensemble of 'palace' architecture.

From 1661 onwards Louis XIV built this most splendid palace in a rather uninspiring swamp outside Paris. As well as enhancing his own personal majesty at Versailles, Louis XIV made an art of court etiquette and ceremonial, diverting the energies of aristocratic and powerful men into harmless channels. With a compliant nobility, Louis XIV was able to rule absolutely ('*L'etat c'est moi*'), and Versailles established itself as the *beau idéal* of the royal palace.

In the eighteenth century Versailles inspired other monarchies to produce a flood of imitations. In Italy, for instance, yet another hunting-box at Stupinigi, outside Turin, was transformed by the architect Filippo Juvarra in 1729, complete with *cour d'honneur*; in the south, the monumental Caserta was laid out with extraordinary vistas and spacious Baroque interiors. The Spanish version at La Granja has a domed church at the centre of its *cour d'honneur*; by contrast, the Oriente Palace in Madrid is not in the Versailles mould at all, representing the move away from Baroque to a more restrained Classicism.

In Britain the eighteenth century saw no royal palace building of any significance, even though the country was becoming increasingly prosperous and powerful. The minor German dynasty on the throne had nothing to compare with the seats of the aristocracy – such as Blenheim, Castle Howard and Chatsworth – until George IV decided to give Britain palaces worthy of a great power, in which he need not be ashamed to entertain emperors.

The Austrian emperors were given the opportunity to surpass Versailles in two elaborate schemes, for the Hofburg and Schönbrunn, designed by Johann Bernhard Fischer von Erlach, the most outstanding Austrian Baroque architect. With typical Habsburg modesty, the chance was not taken; none the less Schönbrunn was built to Fischer von Erlach's second design, with an imposing *cour d'honneur*. The other great builder of the Baroque in Austria, Lukas von Hildebrandt, was responsible for Prince Eugene of Savoy's delightful Viennese garden palaces, the two Belvederes.

Augustus the Strong of Saxony was one of several larger-than-life monarchs of the Baroque period who wished to build a German Versailles. His architect Matthäus Daniel Pöppelmann gave him the Zwinger, a remarkable series of pavilions at Dresden. Pöppelmann's influence can also be seen at Tsarskoye Selo in Russia, a country where Western architecture was embraced with fervour at the beginning of the eighteenth century. Peterhof is the re-creation of Versailles on a suitably large Russian scale by a pupil of Louis XIV's garden designer Le Nôtre, while the Winter Palace was designed by Rastrelli, an Italian émigré born in Paris. In Sweden, a mixture of French and Italian Baroque was also adopted as the style for the royal palace at Stockholm and the summer residence at Drottningholm.

The concept of the royal palace belongs essentially to the eighteenth century when these vast buildings were the centre of court life, buzzing with intrigue and full of people circling around the monarch. After the French Revolution, absolute monarchy and its appropriate setting rather went out of fashion. The nineteenth century saw monarchs leaning more towards cosy retreats away from the empty, echoing enfilades. There was, though, one remarkable exception in the person of Ludwig II, 'the Dream King' of Bavaria, whose mania for building palaces was inspired by Wagnerian legends, the romantic Marie Antoinette and, of course, by *Le Roi Soleil*. Herrenchiemsee was built as a replica of the middle part of Versailles, complete with a *Galerie des Glaces* or 'Hall of Mirrors', the most famous, and most copied, room in any royal palace.

If Tom Paine were to return today he would doubtless be gratified to learn that so many European monarchies have been dismantled in this century. Two World Wars have put paid to some dozen of them – and quite a few palaces for good measure – but ten remain: those of Belgium, Denmark, Great Britain, Liechtenstein, Luxembourg, Monaco, the Netherlands, Norway, Spain and Sweden. Their sovereign rulers still live in palaces, not without a certain style. Among the former ruling dynasties, the Wittelsbachs are still seated at Nymphenburg (with its exquisite pavilions), while Ludwig II's extravagant castles have proved, ironically, to be the basis for Bavaria's flourishing tourist industry. Even – or, perhaps, especially – in Russia the former residences of the Imperial family are maintained in impeccable order. Much of the fabric of the royal palaces of Europe damaged during the Second World War has been restored in almost miraculous fashion.

The palaces have benefited from modern scholarship, the treasures within being rearranged by expert hands, and there has been a new appreciation of their importance to the human heritage. For all Paine's strictures, no egalitarian state can ever achieve a fraction of what the royal families have done for architecture and the arts through their munificent patronage and great collections. Many royal palaces are now once again full of people. They have come not to throw stones but to study and enjoy the splendid background created by those who made history.

France
and Monaco

The first French king from the House of Bourbon, Henri IV, died as he arrived at the Louvre after being stabbed in his carriage by a religious fanatic in May 1610. Earlier in his colourful life, *le Roi galant*, who caused havoc to his wet-nurse by being born with a head full of teeth, had narrowly escaped being assassinated while relieving himself in a pigsty – a Rabelaisian situation fully in keeping with his nature. The Bourbons followed the Valois and Capet dynasties on the French throne, after the Protestant Henri had prudently decided that '*Paris vaut bien une messe*' ('Paris is certainly worth a Mass'), and embraced Catholicism in 1593.

Earlier in the sixteenth century, the medieval palace of the Louvre had been largely demolished by François I (*le Roi Nez*) and rebuilt to the designs of Pierre Lescot, with sculptural decoration by Jean Goujon. In its early days the Louvre was a fortress to protect the city from riverside attack, rather the Parisian equivalent of the Tower of London. By the fourteenth century it had become an official royal residence and one of the towers housed Charles V's celebrated early library of 973 volumes.

François I (r. 1515–47) has more important claims to our attention than his prominent proboscis. A great Renaissance figure, he was a patron of Leonardo da Vinci whom he installed at Amboise, the palace of Charles VIII by the Loire. Da Vinci may have had a hand in the design of the famous spiral staircase at Blois nearby, a brilliant piece of inventiveness and structural virtuosity. François added a wing here in the Italian style and also built the best known of the celebrated *châteaux* of the Loire, Chambord. From 1519 onwards the king's architect, Trinqueau, employed some 1,800 men on this massive project – 440 rooms, 50 staircases – but Chambord was still unfinished at the time of François's death 28 years later. Its best-known feature is one particular internal staircase, which rises from floor to roof in a double spiral. For all its size, François regarded Chambord merely as a hunting-lodge set in a deer park rather than as a royal palace; in the following century Louis XIV expressed the view that it was too small.

At the same time as François I was building this hunting-lodge on a palatial scale, he was also transforming another hunting-lodge, nearer Paris, into what was unquestionably a palace: Fontainebleau. He pulled down most of the original medieval fort, save for the keep, rebuilt the *Cour ovale*, laid out the present main courtyard, and linked the two with the long gallery still known as *La Galerie de François I*. The *Porte dorée*, from which stretches the long avenue into the vast hunting forest, and the *Cour ovale* staircase are architectural examples of the developing understanding of Italian Renaissance theory. François I's chief contribution to the magnificence of Fontainebleau was the interior, where he set a squadron of Italian artists and craftsmen, led by Primaticcio and Rosso Fiorentino, to the task of creating what he called a 'second Rome'. Every available space was filled with frescoes, stucco and marble. François's successors carried on the work at Fontainebleau: Henri II completed the ballroom to the designs of de L'Orme; Charles IX placed the plaster cast of the bronze horse in the *Basse Cour* (which later became known as the *Cour du Cheval blanc*) and Henri IV doubled the size of the palace. 'They

1 (*previous page*) Amboise, on the Loire, is a mixture of various periods. The mighty round tower (on the left) evokes medieval warfare; the main building was begun by Charles VIII (1483–98) and a team of Italian craftsmen, but the sixteenth century saw a typically French 'Mannerist' style being applied to the *château*, complete with dormer windows. Leonardo da Vinci was buried at Amboise; he had been brought here by that great Renaissance monarch, François I.

2 François I's Gallery at Fontainebleau, by the exuberant Florentines Giovanni Battista Rossi and Francesco Primaticcio (the 'First School of Fontainebleau'), with its wooden panelling and friezes of painting and sculpture. Nearly 200 feet long, the Gallery is less than 17 feet wide. Begun in 1531, this was the first room of its kind in a royal palace and was to be much copied.

accuse me of being stingy', *le Roi galant* once complained, 'but I do three things which are far removed from meanness – I make war, I make love and I build.' Henri IV also laid out the Grand Canal here, while the French and Flemish artists he put to work (including Fréminet, Ambroise Dubois and Toussaint Dubreuil) came to be known as the 'Second School of Fontainebleau'.

The patron of the 'First School of Fontainebleau', François I, collected the paintings and treasures that were to be the eventual basis of the Louvre museum. Artists represented in his collection, apart from the immortal da Vinci, included Andrea del Sarto, Raphael and Benvenuto Cellini. The rebuilding of the Louvre along classical lines came at the end of François I's reign and Lescot's work on the west wing demonstrated how much the French Renaissance had absorbed from the Italian.

After François I's death in 1547, Henri II and Lescot continued building at the Louvre. Some of the interior features were surprisingly innovative for that period; a gallery was supported by Goujon's four caryatids – a form almost unheard-of in France in the mid-sixteenth century. For the wooden ceiling of the impressive King's Chamber (where he would receive ambassadors, hold *levée* and *couchée* ceremonies, and eat), Lescot worked with another collaborator. Previous ceilings tended to be of traditional French patterns with beams running across them and painted *motifs*, whereas this creation of Lescot and the Italian wood-carver Scribec de Carpi rivalled the most elaborate designs of the period, even in Venice.

Around the Louvre settled all the impedimenta of state: guards, courtiers, the rest of the nobility who wanted to be close to the king, petitioners and other hangers-on. Henri II was particularly concerned about the outbuildings: his stables had to hold up to 6,000 horses. The king met his end during a tournament arranged to celebrate his daughter's wedding to Philip II of Spain, and the

3 The entrance front of Fontainebleau, looking out on to the *Basse Cour*, was built by François I between 1530 and 1540. This courtyard came to be known as the *Cour du Cheval blanc* when Charles IX placed the plaster cast of a bronze horse here; after Napoleon's farewell to his Guard this name was, in turn, superseded by *Cour des Adieux*. The much-imitated 'Horseshoe Staircase' was built by Louis XIII's architect Jean du Cerceau.

4 The old fourth side of the Louvre complex, the Tuileries Palace, which was gutted by fire during the Commune in May 1871. Begun by Catherine de'Medici to the designs of Philibert de L'Orme in the 1560s, it was transformed by Le Vau for Louis XIV, stormed in the French Revolution (when it became the headquarters of the Convention) and was restored by Napoleon III. After the fire of 1871, the remains were cleared, leaving the Louvre open-ended. The Tuileries Gardens were remodelled by Le Nôtre in the reign of Louis XIV along the French formal lines he made famous.

mantle of royal builder then fell upon his widow, the scheming Regent Catherine de' Medici.

Catherine began the long gallery parallel to the Seine with the idea of joining the Louvre to her new palace of the Tuileries. The architect of the Tuileries, Philibert de L'Orme, did not entirely see eye to eye with his formidable patron, preferring something rather simpler than the rich ornaments and materials close to Catherine's heart, but he did his best to carry out her orders until his death in 1570. Not long afterwards Catherine appears to have abandoned the Tuileries. The necessary building work to link the two palaces was carried on by Henri IV.

The Tuileries did not come into its own until the reign of Louis XIV (1643–1715), when he mounted the memorable spectacle *Le Grand Carrousel* in 1662 to celebrate the birth of his son, *Le Grand Dauphin*. This outrageously theatrical event featured the king costumed as a Roman emperor complete with gold, silver and diamonds while other members of the royal family were dressed as Persians, Indians, Turks and so forth. Fifteen thousand people watched the

pageantry and the queen looked on from a rostrum in front of the Tuileries decorated with *fleurs-de-lys*. Le Vau, the architect of the *Pavillon de Marsan*, remodelled the palace of the Tuileries and the famous gardens were laid out by André Le Nôtre in the formal, balanced style he perfected. Their lay-out can still be appreciated today: the two outer terraces (along the Rue de Rivoli and the Seine) enclose a symmetrical pattern of parterres, fountains, pools, quincunxes, geometric paths and ramps. The gardens are well stocked with seventeenth-century sculptures.

During Louis XIV's minority, indeed until the crafty Italian cardinal died in 1661, the government was in the hands of Mazarin. While he was successful in matters of foreign policy, following the lines established by his late mentor Cardinal Richelieu, Mazarin blundered at home. This was the period of the near-civil war known as the 'Fronde' when the great nobles and the Paris mob were equally turbulent.

5 The axial layout of Versailles with all roads radiating around *Le Roi Soleil*. The garden front was completed by Jules Hardouin-Mansart, by adding the two wings, in 1679; the façade extends to a length of nearly 1,900 feet. The gardens were laid out by Le Nôtre.

It was Louis XIV's memory of the Fronde which gave birth to Versailles. On the one hand, he moved his court there so as to be at a safe distance from the rabble of Paris; on the other, he made his father's small *château* large enough to accommodate all the nobles of the kingdom, so that by having them near him he was able to keep them under control. But what might be called the 'Versailles system' was not fully established until the later part of his reign, when the *château* grew to its present size.

In order to attract his nobles and dominate them, Louis exalted his kingship to a height unequalled by any other European monarch of recent centuries. He was *Le Roi Soleil*, the sun around which the whole universe of French nobility revolved. To raise himself to these heights, he had, first and foremost, his own personality. Contrary to the popular myth, Louis was tall and of splendid physique. While he could not have been called handsome, there was a regal and mysterious air to his dark, slightly Oriental looks and small, half-closed, all-seeing eyes. He had a tremendous dignity and his movements were extraordinarily graceful; he always knew how to say just the right thing. His splendid health and vitality fitted him well for the arduous duties and endless ceremonies of kingship, particularly as he had unlimited self-control and would spare himself no more than he spared others.

To enhance his own personal majesty, Louis built one of the most splendid palaces Europe has ever seen: he also raised court etiquette and ceremonial to a fine art. This again provided a means of keeping his nobles harmlessly occupied. Dukes who in the past would have plotted rebellions now devoted all their energies to vying with one another as to who should have the privilege of holding the right-hand sleeve of the king's shirt while he was dressing, or of removing his *chaise-percée* or commode.

The magic of *Le Roi Soleil* and his court, however, did not depend on majesty alone. Even the most devoted courtier might eventually have found this boring. Louis XIV was not only regal, but charming; though immensely majestic, he was never pompous. He was always dignified, yet he had a sense of humour. And while much of the time at Versailles was spent in stately ceremonial, there was always a great deal of amusement. There was the hunting and shooting – the king, like most Bourbons, was basically an outdoor man, devoted to field sports. There were the *fêtes* and the long evenings of music, gambling and gossip. There were the amorous intrigues in which the king himself took part until, after the death of the queen, he became the strictly faithful husband of the pious and somewhat puritanical Madame de Maintenon, whom he married secretly. Under the latter's influence he mended his morals and became more religious.

With compliant nobility, Louis was able to rule absolutely, making use of great royal servants such as Colbert, but never allowing them to become his masters. From the death of Mazarin until Louis's own death more than half a century later – after a reign of seventy-two years, the longest in European history, save that of Grand Duke Karl Friedrich of Baden – there was never the slightest doubt as to who was the real ruler of France. '*L'état c'est moi*', as well as summing up Louis's own idea of government, tells us precisely how France was

governed in his reign. And though this well-known saying attributed to Louis refers specifically to government, it could also be an expression of how Louis identified himself with the glory of France, just as Napoleon and de Gaulle did in later years – though in their case they regarded themselves as personifying the nation, whereas Louis regarded the nation as an extension of himself. It is nothing unusual for a ruler to identify himself with his country; but to do so to this extent is something peculiarly French.

Identifying himself as he did with France, it added immeasurably to Louis's majesty that France, during his reign, reached the very summit of her greatness. The armies of Condé and Turenne were everywhere victorious; the arts, literature and music flourished. It was the age of Racine and Molière, of Boileau and La Fontaine, of Mansart and Le Nôtre, of Largillière, of Lully and Couperin. It was also a profoundly religious age, when the French Church produced great preachers like Bossuet and Fénélon, as well as the saintly Père La Chaise.

Versailles, perhaps the most superb *ensemble* of buildings, gardens and landscaped parkland in the world, gave the French decorative arts a tremendous boost. Colbert ensured that the materials were French-made and available for export. The Sun King's creation became the *ne plus ultra* of royal palaces; it was the yardstick by which every other royal palace in Europe, or even beyond that continent, was judged. Other rulers would dutifully reproduce their own version of the *Galerie des Glaces* and the grand apartments, seeking to emulate the layout of its grounds.

7 The *Cour de Marbre*, Versailles, whose brick and stone façades represent the outline of the *château* built by Philibert Le Roy for Louis XIII in 1631. The busts, balconies and pediments were added in the late seventeenth century.

In 1682 the court moved from the Louvre to Versailles, though the work was by no means finished. The numbers of people involved give some idea of the place's size: about a thousand courtiers and some four thousand servants lived in the palace, with a further fifteen thousand soldiers quartered in the barracks and stables, as well as the several thousand workmen employed on the building sites for the next thirty years or so. The hundreds of rooms in the palace itself could accommodate upwards of ten thousand people.

What made Louis XIV's achievement all the more remarkable was the unpromising nature of the stage where he put on the production. The Duc de St-Simon had described it as 'the gloomiest and most barren of places; it has no view, no woods, no soil; for it is nothing but marshes and shifting sands'. The story goes that Louis XIV commandeered his team of Le Vau the architect, Le Brun the decorator and Le Nôtre the gardener after they had all been working together on the *château* of Vaux-le-Vicomte for Mazarin's finance minister, Fouquet. The king had been entertained at a lavish banquet here by Fouquet who, like many a powerful subject, had over-reached himself. Louis, taking a dim view of the amount of state money the minister seemed to have squandered on the *château*, had walked out in a huff, arranged for the minister (who had built not wisely but too well) to languish in jail for the rest of his days and set Le Vau, Le Brun and Le Nôtre to outdo themselves at Versailles.

Le Vau retained the original *château* of Louis XIII as the nucleus for his surrounding extensions so that today it still forms the centre block of the palace,

8 (*left*) The celebrated spiral asymmetric staircase at Blois, on the Loire, is a legacy of the Gothic style in the Renaissance wing built at the palace by François I immediately after his accession in 1515.

9 (*above*) Chambord, on the Loire, was François I's favourite residence: a huge palace, ludicrously known as a 'hunting-box', with over 400 rooms. Building work began in 1519 to the designs of Domenico da Cortona and Trinqueau (the architect of Chenonceaux and Blois), but this mightiest of the Loire *châteaux* was never really finished. Louis XIV thought it too small.

10 (*right*) The Louvre, Paris: the 'French Renaissance' façade designed by Pierre Lescot and built from 1546 to 1551. This was the forerunner of the typical French style: the pavilion with columns, the walls between pilasters. The third storey is decorated with reliefs sculpted by Lescot's collaborator, Jean Goujon.

framing the *Cour de Marbre*. The architect's signal contribution to Versailles was the series of terraces. In Louis XIV's book *Manière de montrer les Jardins de Versailles* the king recommended the visitor to

> leave the Château by the hall leading into the *Cour de Marbre* and go out on the terrace. Stay for a moment at the top of the steps and gaze at the way the flowerbeds are laid out, at the ornamental lakes, and at the fountains. . . .

It is indeed from the terrace that Le Nôtre's great scheme can be appreciated in its formal glory. The marshes had been drained, forests shifted and replanted, the Grand Canal cut, water for the thousand fountains channelled from miles away and the burgeoning gardens dotted with sculptures. From the terrace, to the left stands the Orangery; to the right the *Bassin de Neptune*, in line with the *Pièce d'Eau des Suisses*. The lawn, *l'Allée du Tapis vert*, with its quincunx arrangement of trees on either side, stretches out from the *Bassin de Latone* to the *Bassin d'Apollon* (where the sculpted chariot of the sun rises from the water), leading on to the Grand Canal. Here, Louis XIV would give his celebrated evening boating parties, when elegant if unlikely vessels (such as minute frigates) would traverse the mile-long sheet of water as music wafted out from the orchestra hidden on the shore.

12 The ballroom at Fontainebleau was completed in the 1550s by Henri II, principally to the designs of Philibert de L'Orme, with a coffered ceiling and paintings by Niccolò dell'Abbate following on from Primaticcio. The subjects of the paintings were inspired by mythology and the Farnesina frescoes of Raphael. The chimney-piece, with its bronze canephori (modelled after the marbles of the Capitol Museum), has been restored, as the originals were melted down during the Revolution.

The present façade on to the gardens at Versailles is the work of Jules Hardouin-Mansart, who took over from Le Vau after the original architect's death and was kept busy here until his own in 1708. More and more extensions were found to be necessary as the seat of government and the court were transferred from St-Germain to Versailles. Mansart was effectively responsible for the present appearance of Versailles: he designed the *Galerie des Glaces*, the *Grand Commun*, the chapel, the north and south wings, the Orangery (whose size so surprised the Siamese envoys) and the Grand Trianon in the park.

The *Galerie des Glaces* is named after the 17 tall mirrors which reflect the view from the same number of large windows overlooking the park. On the ceiling Le Brun commissioned an allegorical history in gold of the reign of *Le Roi Soleil*; no opportunity was lost to celebrate his majesty at the palace. The north wing houses the chapel and also the opera-house, built for Louis XV by Jacques-Ange Gabriel from 1757 to 1770. It was first used at the time of the wedding of the Dauphin (the future Louis XVI) and Marie Antoinette.

The kings of France who follow the great Louis are something of an anticlimax. Under his great-grandson Louis XV, the country's finances (admittedly heavily undermined by the Sun King's wars) went from bad to worse and the new king proved quite unequal to the job. In his favour, though, it can be said that Louis XV was a man of taste, favouring the Rococo style of decoration at Versailles. He built the delightful Petit Trianon, to the designs of Gabriel, for the later of his two influential mistresses, Madame du Barry.

Although Louis XV's previous mistress, Madame de Pompadour, is reputed to have said '*Après nous le déluge*', the situation in France actually took a turn for the better when Louis XV died and was succeeded by his 19-year-old grandson.

13 (*below*) Fontainebleau: the bedroom of Louis XIV's secret second wife, the pious and somewhat puritanical Madame de Maintenon.

14 (*right*) The Royal Opera at Versailles was designed by Jacques-Ange Gabriel for Louis XV in 1748, but not built until 21 years later for the festivities to mark the marriage of the Dauphin (later Louis XVI) to Marie Antoinette. Its décor was restored in the 1950s.

The new king, Louis XVI, and his exquisite Austrian queen, Marie Antoinette, seemed young, graceful and innocent after the elderly cynicism of the previous régime. There was a breath of hope in the air; court life became idyllic. The sentimental romances of Florian were all the vogue; the days of *Paul et Virginie* were not far off. At the Petit Trianon Marie Antoinette escaped into a charming fantasy world of utterly bogus rural bliss with her specially-built 'hamlet' (rustic without, regal within) and toy farm with its 'Dairy of Cleanliness' and 'Dairy of Preparation' where she could act out the role of milkmaid. She laid out a garden in the 'English' style at the little classical villa and her architect Mique built the Temple of Love, the Rock Pavilion and a small theatre.

However frivolous and pleasure-loving Marie Antoinette may have been in her happier days, the courage with which she faced the fearful trials of the Revolution make her a figure not to be underestimated. Charm is the least communicable of qualities to a sceptical posterity but Marie Antoinette's was sufficient to stop the mob in its tracks when they came to storm Versailles and found her standing on the balcony overlooking the *Cour de Marbre*. They cheered the queen then, but in the end she was to suffer an even worse fate than her husband. Louis XVI went to the guillotine in January 1793 whereas her prison sentence extended to her execution the following October.

15 Malmaison: the Music Room of the Empress Josephine's favourite residence.

The ransacking of the palace by the mob in 1789 was one of the darkest episodes in the history of Versailles, though it would be foolish to pretend that life there was ever quite as paradisal as it might now seem. The human face behind the painted mask has to be borne in mind: the intrigue, the scandals (such as *L'Affaire des Poisons* and *L'Affaire du Collier*), the less than adequate sanitary arrangements. Another black day was the proclamation of Kaiser William I as the German Emperor here in January 1871 after the French had been defeated by the Prussians. The wheel came full circle, however, after the First World War when the Treaty of Versailles was signed in the *Galerie des Glaces* in 1919.

In post-revolutionary France the idea of *la gloire* has, on the whole, conjured up the exploits of Napoleon and his marshals rather than those of Louis XIV and *Le Grand Condé*. Napoleon's favourite royal palace was Fontainebleau; even in his final exile on St Helena he spoke of it as '*la vraie demeure des rois, la maison des siècles*' ('the true dwelling of kings, the house of centuries'). Here, on 20 April 1814, he had descended the great 'horseshoe' staircase in the *Cour du Cheval blanc* (thereafter sometimes known as the *Cour des Adieux*) to bid an emotional farewell to his faithful Guard before being taken away to Elba.

Napoleon found a palace somewhat altered since the days of the Renaissance. Louis XIV had brought in Le Nôtre to design a formal garden; Louis XV had knocked down the *Galerie d'Ulysse* (decorated by Primaticcio) and the *Pavillon des Poëles* (dating from the reign of Henri II) in favour of the new *Gros Pavillon* along the south side of the main courtyard; and the Queen's Apartments (including a Turkish boudoir) had been fitted up for Marie Antoinette. The decorations and the treasures inside had survived the Revolution very well, though the stock of furniture was considerably depleted. Napoleon brought in Empire-style furniture, converted the King's Bedroom to the *Salle du Trône* and introduced the imperial touch to the Grand Apartments. Soon Fontainebleau was enjoying a new lease of life with hunting parties and other jollifications.

16 Compiègne: the façade of the palace facing on to the Place du Palais. The old *château* (where Louis XIV was *en paysan*) was rebuilt in the 1750s by Louis XV to the design of Jacques-Ange Gabriel. The architecture has been described as that of a grand municipal building rather than of a royal palace.

A less agreeable feature of the new occupancy was the use of the palace as a prison for Pope Pius VII. The upstart emperor had achieved the triumph of getting the pope to come to Paris to crown him in the cathedral of Notre-Dame, and duly treated him as an honoured guest. However, during the ceremony, Napoleon rudely snatched the crown out of the pontiffs hands at the last minute and placed it on his own head, then with his own hands crowned Josephine. Pius VII was later confined to his quarters at Fontainebleau, where Napoleon bullied him mercilessly.

Empress Josephine, a dedicated gardener, may have had a hand in the informal *Jardin anglais* at Fontainebleau. Josephine came from Martinique, in the West Indies, but when she married the ambitious Corsican general she was prominent in Parisian society as the widow of the Vicomte de Beauharnais, a French noble of radical tendencies who had ended his life on the guillotine. She created a most attractive garden at Malmaison, where her heart always remained when Napoleon went into the world of the Tuileries and Fontainebleau. Built about 1620 outside the village of Rueil, the *château* was enlarged by Josephine to the designs of Percier and Fontaine at the turn of the nineteenth century. Josephine spent as much time as she could in the stately greenhouse, which had a drawing-room of its own. She collected rare trees and exotic plants from all over the world and entertained many eminent botanists. Malmaison was the scene of what little domestic bliss the Bonapartes enjoyed together. In 1809 they divorced and Josephine returned to Malmaison once more where she died five years later. Today the *château* is a Napoleonic museum.

17 (*left*) The Temple of Love in the *Jardin anglais* of the Petit Trianon at Versailles, which was built for the romantic Marie Antoinette, Louis XVI's queen, by her architect Richard Mique in 1778.

18 (*right*) A salon of the Empress Eugénie at Compiègne which she and Napoleon III filled with the distinctive Second Empire furniture.

The architectural team of Percier and Fontaine also carried out work for Napoleon at the Louvre, completing the link with the Tuileries Palace and beginning the north wing along the Rue de Rivoli. In 1810 Napoleon married the Archduchess Marie Louise, daughter of his vanquished foe the Emperor Franz, and decided to add Compiègne to his collection of official residences. Yet again, the palace north of Paris on the Oise had begun life as a royal hunting-box. Louis XIV once said: '*Je suis logé à Versailles en Roi, à Fontainebleau en Prince et à Compiègne en paysan*' ('I am housed at Versailles like a king, at Fontainebleau like a prince and at Compiègne like a peasant'). It is recorded that this unlikely *paysan* visited Compiègne no less than 75 times. The *château* was turned into a palace by Louis XV and Louis XVI in rather an austere neo-classical style. The architect, J. A. Gabriel of Versailles fame, had a difficult task fitting the rebuilding into a triangular spot. The rising ground obliged him to make three storeys on the town front and two facing the park. The town front has the benefit of a portico and columns, but the garden front is a singularly boring piece of architecture.

Napoleon undertook a thorough renovation of Compiègne, installing his beloved First Empire furniture for his new bride (whose first remark to Napoleon after he had surprised her with a kiss in her carriage was to say 'Sire, your portrait did not flatter you'), and extending the avenue. The idea was to remind the Austrian Archduchess of Schönbrunn.

Compiègne's heyday came in the Second Empire when Bonaparte's nephew Napoleon III and his Empress Eugénie held court here in glittering style. Balls,

20 An engraving of the *Grande Cascade* in the park of St-Cloud, outside Paris, on 1 April 1810 – the day that Napoleon married Archduchess Marie Louise of Austria in the royal palace *(top right)* in a civil ceremony. The cascade is one of the few remains of the great waterworks installed here during the reign of Louis XIV by Francini when St-Cloud was the residence of the king's brother, the Duc d'Orléans. The palace itself was burned down in 1870.

hunting parties, *soirées*, as well as the empress's beloved charades were the order of the day until the Franco-Prussian War brought this slightly pinchbeck period to an end. Towards the end of her long life (she lived until 1920), the Empress Eugénie unwisely returned to the scene of those far-off days, incognito, as a tourist. The guide taking her round did not recognize the former *châtelaine* until an incident in the *Salon des Fleurs* (named after the panels painted by Dubois in 1810). As the Empress entered the room she turned as if by instinct to the architrave on the right of the door leading from the *Grand Salon*. What she saw there reduced her to tears. Pencilled on the woodwork was a line indicating the height of her only child: 'Louis – dix ans'. Louis, the Prince Imperial, had been killed thirteen years afterwards in the Zulu War of 1879. Among the collection of the Empress's belongings in the palace today (now a museum) are the actual *assegais* that ended the hapless youth's life in the service of Queen Victoria.

The British queen was entirely captivated by Napoleon and Eugénie on their state visit to England in 1855 and henceforth rated the French Imperial couple among her dear friends. Victoria, Albert and their two eldest children later came to stay – the first time a reigning sovereign from across the Channel had visited France since 1431 – at St-Cloud. The queen's rooms in the *château* (built in 1675 by Mansart for the Duc d'Orléans, Louis XIV's brother) enjoyed the outlook towards Paris 'the view of which is splendid'. The queen remarked that the furniture at St-Cloud was all 'so charming and so well stuffed, that by lying a little while on the sofa you are completely rested'. Her sitting-room and drawing-room ('quite lovely') overlooked the gardens with their cascades and fountains: 'These regular old gardens', Queen Victoria noted, 'are beautiful and very gay.' In the park the *Grande Cascade* (designed by Le Pautre with additions by Mansart) and the *Jet de la Grande Gerbe* are the only major remains at St-Cloud of the waterworks contrived here by Francini.

Today only a plantation of yews marks the spot where the Château de St-Cloud once stood, but it will always retain its place in French history. Henri III was murdered here by Montgomery in 1589; here Napoleon pulled off his *coup d'état* in 1799 and also married for the second time in 1810; here Charles X provoked the 'July Revolution' of 1830 by his breezy 'Four Ordinances of St-Cloud'. The *château* finally went up in smoke in 1870 during the Franco-Prussian War.

In the following year, during the Commune, the Tuileries Palace was also gutted by fire. The remains were razed to make way for a garden and so the Louvre took on its present open-ended appearance. The royal palaces of France that have survived are now all museums. The last Bourbon monarch, the 'Citizen King' Louis Philippe (who in the revolution of 1848 was obliged to slip away in a hackney-cab under the assumed name of 'Mr William Smith'), saved Versailles from demolition by turning it into a museum dedicated to '*Toutes les Gloires de la France*'.

21 The *Palais Princier*, Monaco: the main entrance showing the contrast between the Genoese fortifications and the eighteenth-century building. The arms of the House of Grimaldi are above the doorway protected by the Monégasque guard. Cannons are a special feature of the palace – on the north and south sides they are placed beside pyramids of cannonballs, recalling its days as a fortress.

22 (*above*) 'I, Monaco, on my rock': the *Palais Princier* is in the centre foreground; the pedimented building on the cliff's edge, in the background, is the Oceanographic Museum founded by Prince Albert I in 1906.

23 (*right*) The Mazarin Room of the *Palais Princier* takes its name from the portrait of the Cardinal who was chief minister to the young Louis XIV. The polychrome *boiseries* are seventeenth-century.

In the spring of 1815 Prince Honoré-Gabriel of Monaco, who had served in the Napoleonic Army throughout most of its campaigns and had done a stint as Grand Equerry to the Empress Josephine, was on his way back to take charge of the principality on behalf of his uncle Prince Honoré IV when he was stopped by a party of armed men outside Cannes. At the head of this posse was General Cambronne, who recognized the prince and led him to an olive grove, where, at a camp fire, sat Napoleon, just back from Elba.

'Well, where are you going?' said the emperor.

'To take possession of my territories again, in Monaco', replied the prince.

'Me too, in Paris.'

Honoré-Gabriel found the principality in a sorry state. The town of Monaco having been besieged, captured and sacked at the time of the Revolution, the palace had been plundered of all its treasures and used successively as a prison, an asylum and a barracks. Originally a fortress, it was occupied by the Holy Imperial troops when the Grimaldis first came on the scene as outlaws from Genoa in the late thirteenth century.

The story goes that Lanfranco Grimaldi (known as 'The Spiteful') succeeded in capturing the fortress by arriving one evening disguised as a friar and begging shelter for the night. Having thus gained admittance to the fortress, he drew the sword which he had concealed under his habit, and fell on his unfortunate hosts after they had gone to bed. The Spiteful then opened the castle gates to the band of warriors whom he had brought with him. There, give or take a warlike interruption by the Genoese, the Grimaldis remained.

During the next five centuries, the Grimaldi lords of Monaco were from time to time under the protection of the French kings; but at other times they allied themselves to the House of Anjou, to the Republics of Florence and Genoa, to the Papacy, to Savoy and to Spain. In return for protection, they usually had to cede a part of their territory, which was thus gradually reduced. Long before Monaco had shrunk to its present size, it became a source of wonder how the little country managed to keep going. '*Son Monaco sopra uno scoglio, Non semino et non raccoglio, E pur mangiare voglio*', became a familiar saying – 'I, Monaco, on my rock, I neither sow nor reap, yet I wish to eat'.

At the beginning of the seventeenth century, Honoré II, the first of the dynasty to assume the princely style and dispense with his surname in official documents, switched his alliance from the declining Spanish Empire back to the original patrons of his family, the kings of France, who were now on their way to becoming the most powerful sovereigns in Europe. He was, in consequence, made a peer of France and Duc de Valentinois; while his grandson and successor, Louis I, was recognized as Prince of Monaco and accorded the rank and prerogatives of a *prince étranger* at the French court. From now until 1817, Monaco remained under the protection of France.

It was Prince Honoré II who transformed the old castle into a royal palace. The castle had been enlarged in the fourteenth century, given a state hall (now the guard-room) in the fifteenth and greatly improved in the sixteenth to the extent that the Emperor Charles V spent four days here en route to his coronation in 1529. Later in the sixteenth century the Milanese architect Dominique Gallo added two storeys of arcaded galleries along the south (the State Rooms wing) and had frescoes painted by Luca Cambiase.

With a view to making the place look less like a fortress, Honoré II commissioned the Genoese architect Jacques Cantone to add decorative embellishments to the main façade. A suite of drawing-rooms was tacked on to the State Rooms wing and the first-floor balcony was adorned with frescoes of *The Labours of Hercules* by Orazzio Ferrari. Other new features included a chapel

24 The *Cour d'Honneur* of the *Palais Princier*, Monaco. The twin marble staircase, an imitation of the Horseshoe Staircase at Fontainebleau, was built by Prince Louis I (who reigned from 1662 to 1701) to the design of Antoine Grigho from Como.

with a cupola and a French-style garden, complete with a summerhouse (the Bath Pavilion which was wrecked in the French Revolution). Inside Ferrari painted the fresco of Alexander the Great in the Grimaldi (or Throne) Room and the palace was filled with a fabulous collection of treasures by Honoré II, including several portraits by Titian.

Honoré II's successors continued to enhance the palace's splendour. Louis I built a great doorway surmounted by a pediment bearing the princely arms and also constructed the Fontainebleau-style twin marble staircase. In the early eighteenth century the Royal Room was decorated by Gregorio de Ferrari and Alexandre Haffner with figures of Fame and the Four Seasons. The Royal Bedchamber was renamed the York Room after Edward, Duke of York, had paid an unscheduled visit in 1767 when illness forced him to land in the principality. The old sea-dog died here; and, in return for easing his brother's last hours, George III invited Honoré III over to the British court where the

Monégasque prince was accorded the honours due to a sovereign.

After the depredations of the French Revolution, the *Palais Princier* was sympathetically restored, though its fine contents had been dispersed. Among the new features were frescoes in the chapel and also on the main façade; the latter depicted the past glories of the Grimaldis and of the principality. The restoration work was completed by Charles III who rebuilt St Mary's Tower and remodelled the guard room in the Renaissance manner, complete with a vast chimney-piece. He also set about retrieving some of the palace's treasures. Happily a fair percentage of the pictures were recovered, including *The Music Lesson* by Titian and Louis Lagrenée's *Love's Education*.

In 1861 Charles III brought Monaco back once again under the wing of France, after an awkward period warding off the attentions of the ever-acquisitive House of Savoy. One of the by-products of the agreement, whereby France recognized Monaco as a sovereign state, was the coming of the railway and the Corniche. Suddenly Monaco was transformed from being a remote and impoverished principality – derisively called 'a rock and an orangery' – into the playground of Europe. So quickly and in such numbers did the patrons flock to the new casino that by the mid-1860s the new town of Monte Carlo had to be built to accommodate them. The revenues were so great by 1869 that Charles III was able to make himself more than ever popular with his fortunate subjects by exempting them from all rates and taxes.

The contents of the *Palais Princier* were enriched in this century by the Napoleonic collection of Prince Louis II, whose mother (*née* Douglas-Hamilton) was the granddaughter of Stephanie de Beauharnais. Also through the Scottish ducal house of Hamilton the Grimaldis inherited some objects from the great English collector William Beckford, the 'caliph of Fonthill'. Louis I's grandson and successor, Prince Rainier III, has, like several other twentieth-century monarchs, shown a keen interest in stamps, reflected in the Stamp Museum at the palace.

The present stylish condition of the interior and the lush gardens owe much to the late Princess Grace, who played her part in real life as well as she played a princess on celluloid in *The Swan*. The American film-star brought a special glamour to the Principality, making the *Palais Princier* the focal point of life in a place that enjoys a uniquely fashionable reputation. The concerts which Prince Rainier and Princess Grace began holding in the main courtyard of the palace were soon established as a noted feature of the Monégasque calendar.

Russia

25 (*previous page*) Peterhof: Rastrelli's armorial
pavilion, with its gilt Baroque dome. To top it off
the architect added the heraldic weather-vane. (*See
pages 41, 44*)

26 (*below*) The Winter Palace, St Petersburg: the
Neva front, which is over 500 feet long and 100
feet high. The palace was rebuilt four times. Its
principal architect was Bartolomeo Rastrelli, who
carried out the major rebuilding programme in
the mid-1750s for the Empress Elisabeth.

It is a well-known paradox that the Communists who evicted the Imperial House
of Russia in the revolution of 1917 now maintain the former royal palaces with
remarkable care and devotion. In St Petersburg (now Leningrad), the Winter
Palace has become the great Hermitage Museum; outside the city, Peterhof or
Petrodvorets (the 'Russian Versailles') has been restored since its devastation by
the Nazis in the Second World War, likewise Tsarskoye Selo (now Pushkin) and
Pavlovsk. In Moscow, of course, the Kremlin is still the Kremlin.

St Petersburg was founded on the banks of the mighty River Neva in 1705 by
Tsar Peter I, who later proclaimed himself Emperor and Autocrat of All the
Russias and is known to history as 'Peter the Great'. The House of Romanoff
had acceded to the Russian throne nearly a hundred years earlier after the 'time of
troubles'. In this period the throne had been occupied by a number of usurpers
and pretenders, and Russia was invaded by Poland. This unruly state of affairs
was settled by the election in the National Council of Mikhail Romanoff as Tsar
in 1613. The Romanoffs, a leading Boyar dynasty, had come to prominence in
1547 when Anastasia Romanovna Zakharin-Koshkin (a great-aunt of Mikhail
Romanoff) married the penultimate ruler of the House of Rurik, 'Ivan the
Terrible'. Peter the Great was Tsar Mikhail's grandson.

Peter, a practical man with a lively grasp of the essentials, preferred his
architects to come from northern parts. Thus the first Winter Palace, a modest
two-storeyed building with a slate roof, on the canal (Winter Dike) linking the
Neva with the Moika River, was built in his favourite Dutch style in 1711. The
second version of the Winter Palace, with a central projecting pediment, was
built in 1721 by the German architect Georg Johann Mattarnovi, who came to
Russia with Andreas Schlüter (designer of the Berlin Schloss). Although this
new house overlooked the Neva itself, it was of fairly modest dimensions until
doubled in size by the Swiss-Italian Domenico Tressini, who was also involved
in the plans for the cathedral and other buildings in the swiftly expanding city.

Peter the Great died here in 1725, but his young son Peter II moved the capital
to Moscow during his brief reign. When the Empress Anna (Peter the Great's
niece) returned to St Petersburg in 1732, she found the Winter Palace not nearly
grand enough for her imperial majesty and took up residence next door at the
much smarter house of Count Apraxine. Anna's revamped Winter Palace was
designed by the Italian Bartolomeo Rastrelli, known as *Il Magnifico*,
incorporating another house from the northern side of Palace Square.

In the reign (beginning 1741) of the Empress Elisabeth (Peter the Great's only
surviving daughter, who married the field-marshal son of a Cossack shepherd),
Rastrelli became Russia's leading architect, carrying out all the major court
commissions. The son of a sculptor who came to Russia in 1715, Rastrelli had
gained valuable experience touring around Europe, particularly Paris and
southern Germany. His style is closest in character to the late Baroque of central
Europe, as exemplified by Lukas van Hildebrandt, the architect of the Belvedere
in Vienna. After Elisabeth's accession, Rastrelli continued to tinker with the
ever-increasing pile beside the Neva; but then the architect came to the
conclusion that it was time to start afresh. In 1753 he presented the empress with
his designs for a new Winter Palace.

27 The Winter Palace: the Gallery of 1812. To commemorate the Russian triumph over Napoleon, Tsar Alexander I commissioned this neo-Classical chamber in 1862 by Carlo Rossi. The pictures are of the war heroes; the equestrian Tsar himself is portrayed at the end.

The old palace was duly demolished a year later and building operations carried on until after Empress Elisabeth's death in 1759. The first resident, in 1762, was her nephew Peter III who installed himself and his mistress Countess Vorontsova in the first floor, packing off his German wife Catherine to the west wing. This formidable female was not to stay there long: after Catherine had been humiliated in front of a large dinner-party she vowed revenge. With the help of her favourite, Grigory Orloff, she staged a *coup d'état* on 9 July; eight days later Peter III was murdered.

Catherine coolly ascended the throne herself where she earned the sobriquet of 'Great' previously conferred on her grandfather-in-law. She installed Orloff in her part of the palace and used the west wing for the Petersburg deliberations of the new legislative commission.

Catherine the Great lent a Palladian touch to the Winter Palace, through her architects Starov and Quarenghi. This Classical style was carried further in the early nineteenth century by the architect Carlo Rossi, who built a gallery for the heroes of the 1812 war against Napoleon.

Catherine the Great, though unscrupulous in her methods, was 'enlightened' in her ideas. The whim of building a Hermitage beside the Winter Palace was derived from J.-J. Rousseau, that promoter of the simple life. Vallin de la Mothe built Catherine a pavilion, linked to her main apartments, where she would entertain friends such as Diderot and Grimm on condition that they had 'to leave their dignity at the door, together with their hats and swords'.

The art collection of the Imperial family also gathered momentum in Catherine's reign and, to accommodate its overflow from the palace, further buildings were added to the Hermitage complex nearby.

The gigantic proportions of the Winter Palace (100 feet high, more than 500 feet long and containing an alleged 1,500 rooms, and over 100 staircases) have to be viewed in relationship to the vastness of the stage on which it is set. The north front, now coloured green and white, looks across the expansive waters of the Neva to the Fortress of SS Peter and Paul. Rastrelli's plan was to make the exterior orange and white; but after the fire of 1837 Nicholas I's architects Stasov and Bryullov gave it a red-brick colouring. The façade is decorated by two ranges of white columns and the balustrade is surmounted by a variety of Baroque statues and urns. The south front, which is similar in design, faces on to the Palace Square, where it forms a splendid ensemble with Rossi's building of the War Ministry. The two lateral fronts are hidden from view; the east adjoins the Hermitage and the west encloses a garden designed in the reign of the stern Nicholas I, who suppressed the insurrection of 1825.

The fire of 1837, which started in the heating shaft of the Hall of Field-Marshals, did lasting damage to much of the interior of the Winter Palace, though Stasov and Bryullov restored the state rooms as faithful replicas of the originals. The outstanding feature to remain as it was built is Rastrelli's Staircase of the Ambassadors (or Jourdain Staircase) which leads down to the main entrance on the Neva front. Every Epiphany, the Tsars would descend this great Baroque staircase on their way to the ceremony of Blessing the Waters, when the river was given Imperial benediction.

Among the hundreds of gilded and pillared galleries, ballrooms and saloons in the Winter Palace are the Treasury Room, containing the Romanoff regalia; the Nicholas Room, scene of court balls; the Peter the Great Room, where diplomats used to assemble on New Year's Day to pay their respects to the Emperor; and the Room of the Order of St George, where the first Douma or Imperial Parliament was opened.

The other Imperial residence in St Petersburg, the Michael Palace, was built by Catherine the Great's son, the Emperor Paul, from 1797 by Bazhenov to designs by Vincenzo Brenna. The site, bordered by the Moika and Fontanka Rivers, had previously been occupied by a wooden summer palace built for the Empress Elisabeth by Rastrelli in the 1740s and was in fact where Paul was born in 1754. Apparently the Archangel Michael figured in a dream of Paul's, telling him to build a church on his birthplace. Paul duly obliged, knocking down Rastrelli's attractive summer palace and building not only a church but a castle which was appropriately finished on the Feast of the Archangel Michael in 1800. Its construction – a classical eighteenth-century building with a portico and Ionic columns, defended like a medieval fortress with moats and drawbridges – reflected a strange and frightened personality.

Paul had returned the remains of his murdered father, Peter III, to the Armorial Hall at the Winter Palace; he detested the crimes which he had seen his mother commit. Strongly wedded as he was to legitimacy, the Emperor Paul, in the days of the Consulate, admired Napoleon, of whom he would say, 'I have found a man; there is a man in the world!' The key to his contradictory nature seems to lie in the fact that he had secret doubts about the divine concept of monarchy which he so rigorously upheld. Being unsure of his convictions made him unhappy and consequently all the more violent and tyrannical in his behaviour. He became highly unpopular and lived in fear of assassination (hence the drawbridges and so on). As is the case with many paranoiacs, his fears were far from groundless. There was indeed a plot to dethrone him – the last of those palace revolutions that are such a feature of Russian history up to the beginning of the nineteenth century. It had the approval of Paul's son, the Tsarevich Alexander, who was assured by the conspirators, led by the Governor-General of St Petersburg, Count Pahlen, that nothing worse would happen to the emperor than imprisonment. This was genuinely the intention of some of them; but when they attempted to seize the unfortunate Paul inside the Michael Palace, they were afraid that his cries would bring the palace guards to his rescue so they put him to death. Forty days after Paul had moved into his stronghold in 1801 he was smothered in his bed.

The room where he gasped his last was preserved later in the nineteenth century as a chapel. By that time the Michael Palace, which remained empty until 1823, had long since been the Military Engineering Academy. One of its students was the young Dostoyevsky.

The Michael Palace should not be confused with the Mikhail (or Mikhailovsky) Palace built for the Emperor Paul's youngest son, Grand Duke Mikhail, from 1819 by Rossi. A Neapolitan by birth, Rossi had been brought up in Russia where he became the last of the great Neo-Classical designers. He gave the Mikhail Palace a large portico with eight Corinthian columns, and a broad loggia with twelve columns at the back. The Grand Duchess Elena Pavlovna, a princess of Württemberg, who married the Grand Duke Mikhail in 1824, shortly before the palace was completed, held a brilliant salon here.

At the end of the nineteenth century the Mikhail Palace was converted into the 'Russian Museum of Emperor Alexander III'. The idea behind the museum was to shift the purely Russian portion – icons and early Christian paintings, among other items – of the Tsars' great art collection into one place. Today it is still called the Russian Museum (though without the addition of the genitive clause) and still houses folk art.

After the Emperor Paul's smothering at the Michael Palace in 1801, his son Alexander I returned to the Winter Palace which remained the home of the Imperial family for most of the nineteenth century. Meanwhile, much of Moscow had been devastated by Napoleon. The Kremlin, however, remained the place where the Tsars were crowned. In the 1830s Nicholas I decided to commission a new palace to replace the rather unsatisfactory collection of buildings he was obliged to use on his visits there. The Emperor Nicholas was a man who knew his own mind; for instance, when he was consulted by engineers as to the course of the projected railway from St Petersburg to Moscow, he took a ruler and drew a straight line between the two capitals. With the same single-mindedness almost all the old palace buildings of the Kremlin, save for the Terem, were razed to clear the way for the new Grand Kremlin Palace, completed in 1849 to the designs of Konstantin Thon.

The Kremlin covered a site of some nine acres and the Grand Palace itself could apparently accommodate 20,000 people in its 700 or so apartments. Today most of the historic buildings in the citadel are museums where the visitor can enjoy such items as the old throne of Boris Godunov.

The brooding monstrosity of the Kremlin in Moscow is a far cry from the 'Russian Versailles' of Peterhof, a dozen miles outside St Petersburg on the Gulf of Finland. Here Peter the Great and his French architect Jean-Baptiste le Blond laid out the basis of a delightful ensemble of park and palaces following a visit to Versailles by the Tsar in 1717. Peter, an inveterate nautical man, had built a small seaside house on the site at the beginning of the century when he was supervising the construction of the fortress at Kronstadt across the water. The first priority in the master plan to emulate Versailles was to find a good source of water for the all-important fountains—above all, to locate a 'Grand Cascade'. The story goes that one day, on a walk with his nobles on a hill about five miles inland, the Emperor divined water. Le Blond was put to work immediately; a reservoir and pipes were installed and the Great Palace was built above the cascade which now disgorged itself from the side of the hill.

The Great Palace at Peterhof, as designed by Le Blond, was hardly comparable to Versailles: it was a straightforward two-storey structure with wings. Peter's seaside residence Monplaisir was more on a par with Marie Antoinette's toy farm, though in this case it was not mere affectation. For during his arduous training for kingship Peter had worked as a shipbuilder on the wharves of Saardam (among other places, including Deptford) and this modest

28 Rossi's neo-Classical Mikhail (or Mikhailovsky) Palace, St Petersburg, built for the Emperor Paul's youngest son Grand Duke Mikhail between 1819 and 1825. Many of the reliefs which decorate the yellow building were by Pimenov and Demut-Malinovsky.

red-bricked house, rusticated in white, recalled his Dutch experience. Inside, reminiscent of a Vermeer, Monplaisir has a hall paved with black and white marble chequers, panelled with oak and hung with Dutch seascapes. The kitchen is panelled with the familiar blue and white Delft tiles, and stocked with pewter dishes and coloured glass bottles. Peter's camp bed, in the whitewashed bedroom, is covered with a patchwork quilt made up by his wife with off-cuts from her dresses.

Le Blond's fountains were the *pièce de résistance*; the Grand Cascade was given a grotto, two lateral cascades, a horseshoe basin and a canal; Samson was sculpted tearing open a lion's jaws to release a spray of water which rose high above the roof of the Grand Palace. The Frenchman actually died in 1719, some years before his vision had become a reality; the fountains, for example, were not operational until 1721. After Peter's death, Peterhof's progress passed through the doldrums until his daughter the Empress Elisabeth put the great Rastrelli in charge.

Rastrelli remodelled Le Blond's Great Palace, adding another storey and doubling its length so that it became twice the width of the Grand Cascade. He also placed single-storeyed galleries at the end of the wings; one a church, the other an armorial pavilion. Both were surmounted by a gilt Baroque dome; the church was topped with a cross, the pavilion with an heraldic weather-vane (the three double-headed eagles of the Romanoffs). The singularity of the church dome offended the Orthodox hierarchy – five was the favoured number – so architectural symmetry had to be sacrificed to religious convention. But the story does not end there as, when the Nazis were here in the Second World War, they destroyed (among almost everything else) the five domes in the church. The Soviet authorities painstakingly restored Peterhof (renamed Petrodvorets or 'Peter's Palace'), turning the church into a post office, though a post office with a difference – for above it was placed a single dome with a cross.

The Empress Elisabeth and Rastrelli also collaborated as patron and architect on the blue and white Baroque Catherine Palace at Tsarskoye Selo (the village of the Tsars). This was named after Elisabeth's mother, Catherine Skavronsky, the widow of a Swedish dragoon and Peter the Great's second wife who succeeded him as Empress in 1725. Like so many royal palaces, it began as a hunting-lodge: a small stone house with a Dutch garden built by his wife in 1718 as a surprise for Peter during one of his many foreign trips. Their daughter Elisabeth was determined to transform it into a fine summer palace but despite employing numerous architects in the 1740s she could not hit upon the right formula. 'It was', wrote Catherine the Great, 'like the task of Penelope. The work of today was all destroyed on the morrow.'

At last, in 1752, Elisabeth made up her mind and gave Bartolomeo Rastrelli his head. *Il Magnifico* indulged himself in golden decorative touches to such an extent on the balustrade above the mammoth façade that the local peasants thought the whole roof was made of gold. The proportions of the Catherine Palace make those of the Winter Palace seem rather restrained; the entrance front of 1,000 feet has a pavilion at one end and a golden-domed church (by Chevakinski) at the other. Inside, Rastrelli provided the Empress Elisabeth with

29 The Catherine Palace, Tsarskoye Selo: the Green Dining-Room. This is one of the first works in Russia by the Scottish architect Charles Cameron, and was carried out between 1780 and 1782 for Catherine the Great. The stucco bas-reliefs are by Martos.

such apartments as the Silver Room, the Great Gallery (shades, once more, of the *Galerie des Glaces*) and the delicious Amber Room, panelled in golden yellow Persian amber. This commodity had been given to Peter the Great when he was in Berlin in 1717 by Frederick William I; upon expressing his admiration for the amber, Peter was told by the Prussian that he could have it 'in exchange for 80 tall recruits'. Sadly, this is one aspect of the palace that the Soviet authorities have not been able to restore since the Nazi depredations.

After the Baroque and Rococo of Elisabeth and Rastrelli came the Classicism of Catherine the Great and Charles Cameron. The latter, originally a protégé of Lord Bute's, had made his name with a book on the Roman Baths and was to

30 The Catherine Palace, Tsarskoye Selo: Cameron's Blue Drawing-Room, with its silk walls and blue floral patterns.

become Catherine's favourite architect. Catherine spent her summers at Tsarskoye Selo from 1763 onwards and decided to set about toning down the exuberance she found there. Rastrelli's gilded plasterwork was repainted in bronze; the statues and urns were removed from the 'gold' roof. The Classical Scot transformed the east wing in his best Adamesque manner: Pompeian frescoes, Wedgwood medallions and so forth. Cameron's Blue Room was nicknamed 'the snuff box' on account of its similarity in design to that receptacle.

Apart from redecorating the Catherine Palace at Tsarskoye Selo, Cameron also made important contributions outside from 1779 to 1792, building the Agate Pavilion (with its exquisite medallions and bas-reliefs by the French sculptor Rachette), the colonnade and various buildings in the park – notably what is now called the Cameron Gallery. The colonnade contains bronze busts of eminent men from antiquity. It is somewhat startling to come across the features of the Whig politician Charles James Fox sandwiched between Demosthenes and Cicero. 'With his eloquence', explained Catherine the Great, 'he had prevented England from making war on Russia. I have no other way of expressing my gratitude. Pitt will be jealous.'

31 Pavlovsk: the Grecian Hall designed by Charles Cameron in the early 1780s, with Corinthian columns in *verde antico*, for the difficult Grand Duchess Maria Feodorovna.

In the early 1780s Cameron took a break from Tsarskoye to design a Palladian palace at Pavlovsk, a few miles away, for Catherine's ill-fated son Paul and his wife Maria Feodorovna. The Scot seems to have had a rough ride from Maria Feodorovna who kept on commissioning other architects; but Cameron's sound basic plan managed to survive a major alteration by Brenna (the designer of the Michael Palace) and other indignities, such as fires and war damage, so that we can still appreciate the great man's work. Pavlovsk is yellow with a distinctive green dome, Corinthian columns and a frieze. Cameron's delicate side-galleries and pavilions were rather clumsily extended into two curved wings by Brenna. Inside, Brenna's militaristic Egyptian Vestibule sits uneasily with Cameron's Italian Hall (under its cupola) and the magnificent Grecian Hall, which has been compared to Robert Adam's Hall at Kedleston in Derbyshire (built for the Curzons some twenty years earlier). The name of Versailles is invoked again in the apartments of Paul and Maria Feodorovna and, of course, in the park with its various temples, monuments and pavilions.

While Pavlovsk was a present for Paul from his mother Catherine the Great, the Alexander Palace back at Tsarskoye Selo was commissioned for her grandson, the future Alexander I. Quarenghi built this yellow and white palace from 1792 to 1796 along austerely Classical lines that are in striking contrast to the curves of its Baroque neighbour. As it turned out Alexander I, who took a great delight in the beauties of nature, preferred the Catherine Palace, though his brother Nicholas I spent much of his time at the Alexander Palace.

When he was Tsarevich, the future Alexander III (who saw his father Alexander II mortally wounded by a Nihilist bomb in 1881) also lived at the Alexander Palace. This large and powerfully-built Tsar, with his beard, his loud voice and his rather terrifying eyes, seemed the very reincarnation of the Russian Bear. Queen Victoria never forgave him for having brought about the overthrow of the young ruler of Bulgaria, Prince Alexander of Battenberg; it was of Alexander III that she made her celebrated remark: 'He may be an *Emperor* but the Queen does *not* regard him as a *gentleman*.'

But however bad Alexander III's image may have been outside Russia, he was popular with the great majority of his subjects. He pleased the more aggressively Russian among them by his policy of Russianization – which included making Russian the official language of the German-speaking Baltic provinces. Alexander liked to think of himself as a Russian peasant, and affected a rough simplicity in his clothes and way of life – though he was the patron of Fabergé. He spent much of his time at a modest house in the country, though this was partly for reasons of security, partly by choice. Ever since the murder of Alexander II, there had been the most elaborate security measures to protect the Tsar and his family, who were consequently seen much less by their subjects. Nevertheless, Alexander III and the Empress Marie were never recluses like their son and daughter-in-law. The beautiful and vivacious empress, who was a Danish princess and the sister of Alexandra, the Princess of Wales, was very popular in Russian society.

It was a tragedy for the Imperial House, for Russia and for the world that Alexander III died in 1894, when he was barely fifty. Had he lived for twenty or

32 The Winter Palace, St Petersburg: the Jourdain Staircase (or Staircase of the Ambassadors). This is the most important survival from Bartolomeo Rastrelli's original interior of the 1754 rebuilding; much of the rest was badly damaged in the fire of 1837. The grey granite columns (to the top of the picture), however, were mid-nineteenth-century additions.

33 Tsarskoye Selo: the Agate Pavilion, built in 1783 by Charles Cameron.

34 (*overleaf left*) The plans for the 'Russian Versailles', Peterhof, were laid out by Peter the Great and his French architect Jean-Baptiste le Blond following a visit to France in 1717. Here a gold Samson can be seen tearing open a lion's jaws to release a jet of water. The Great Palace was considerably enlarged later in the eighteenth century by Rastrelli.

35 (*overleaf top right*) Tsarskoye Selo: one end of the vast Catherine Palace, showing Chevakinski's golden-domed chapel. Originally a hunting-lodge, the Catherine Palace was enlarged to a length of 1,000 feet by the Empress Elisabeth's architect Rastrelli, who was given a free hand in 1752. Later, the Scottish architect Charles Cameron toned down some of the Italian's excessive flourishes.

36 (*overleaf bottom right*) Oranienbaum, on the coast not far from Peterhof, was the setting for palaces built for Peter III (murdered in 1762, having been deposed by his wife Catherine the Great). This is the Chinese Palace designed by Rinaldi for Catherine. Oranienbaum was the only one of the country palaces outside St Petersburg to escape German occupation in 1941.

thirty years longer, his toughness, ability and realism might have saved Russia from the calamities that befell her during the first two decades of this century. Instead, the unwieldy Empire passed to his 26-year-old son, the amiable but weak Nicholas II. Had Nicholas been married to a friendly and warm-hearted princess like his mother, all might have been well with him; but the Empress Alexandra was even more withdrawn from the world than he was.

For most of her husband's reign, Alexandra refused to appear in public or to perform any of the duties of an empress. Her behaviour can to a certain extent be explained by her desperate anxiety over her only son, the Tsarevich Alexis, who was frequently in danger of death and very often in agony owing to the haemophilia which he had inherited from her side of the family. It was her belief that the so-called 'holy man' could cure Alexis which led to her friendship with Rasputin. But even before Alexis was born, she had virtually become a recluse. Such was the Tsar's devotion to her and his own reserve that it was all too easy for him to stay with her in her seclusion. Father, mother and children became entirely self-contained; they led a quiet, rather dull family life in a plainly-furnished corner of the vast and glittering Winter Palace.

After the uprising in 1905, the last Tsar left the Winter Palace rather in the same way that Louis XIV decamped from the Louvre after the *Fronde*. From then on the Imperial family followed a pattern of spending the winter at Tsarskoye Selo (with just the odd night in St Petersburg); May, at a villa on the Peterhof estate; June, cruising in the Imperial yacht in the fjords of Finland; August, at a hunting lodge in the Polish forest; September, on the beaches of the Crimea; and then back to Tsarskoye Selo.

In the Crimea, the Empress Alexandra rebuilt the Livadia Palace in an Italianate style with courtyards and columned balconies commanding spectacular views over the Black Sea beyond the cliffs below. Blessed by Orthodox priests on its opening in April 1911, the white limestone building replaced the old wooden structure where Alexander III had died in 1894. For all the Empress's elaborate touches, Livadia was very much a holiday home where the Imperial family could relax. In its heyday, the white State Dining-Room was sometimes used for dances; in 1945 the infamous Yalta conference, when Roosevelt and Churchill handed Eastern Europe on a plate to 'Uncle Joe', was held here around a circular table.

The Alexander Palace at Tsarskoye Selo was the family's real home from 1905 onwards. Here the Empress had her celebrated mauve boudoir, with everything either mauve or white. Nicholas and Alexandra lived on the ground floor of the east wing; their children on the first floor. A dozen years later the palace was to become the Imperial family's prison, the first in a bewildering series that was to lead to the bloody cellar at Ekaterinburg, where Nicholas, Alexandra, their 13-year-old son and four young daughters were butchered by the Bolsheviks in July 1918.

Three months later the Winter Palace was stormed by the Red Army – an event that still plays an emotional part in Soviet mythology.

Austria and Liechtenstein

37 (*previous page*) The early-nineteenth-century Gothic castle, known as Franzensburg, in the lake at Laxenburg, south of Vienna. Laxenburg, with its statues, cascades, temples and extensive parkland, was a popular retreat for the Imperial Court. (*See page 67*)

38 (*right*) The Baroque Great Gallery at Schönbrunn, Vienna, which runs along the length of the central portion of the entrance front. The ceiling frescoes, depicting Austria-Hungary in war, the arts and the sciences, are by Gregorio Guglielmi.

The sonorous roll-call of the titles held by the last Habsburg ruler, Karl I— Emperor of Austria, Apostolic King of Hungary, King of Bohemia, of Dalmatia, of Croatia, of Slavonia, of Galicia, of Lodomeria, of Illyria, and so on—reflects the ubiquity of the territories acquired by the Habsburgs, mostly by judicious marriages, over the centuries. The name of the dynasty derives from the medieval castle of Habsburg (*Habichtsburg* or 'Hawk's Castle'), built at Aargau in Switzerland by the son of Lanzelin, Count of Altenburg (who died in 991). The Hofburg palace, in the heart of Vienna, became the main stronghold of the Habsburgs in the late thirteenth century when they were still fairly unimportant. Albert, son of Rudolf I of Habsburg (elected King of the Romans in 1273), was the first of the family to become Duke of Austria. From the fifteenth century the Holy Roman Emperors were always Habsburgs except for a brief period in the eighteenth century.

Very little survives of the medieval Hofburg, most of whose rather ungainly buildings date from the reign of the last Habsburg in the male line, Charles VI, in the early eighteenth century. The older parts of this assortment of edifices grouped around courtyards include the medieval *Schweizerhof* and the dignified late-seventeenth-century Leopold Building opposite. Charles VI had imperial ideas for the Hofburg, and commissioned Johann Fischer von Erlach, the master of the Austrian Baroque style, to remodel the place on a grand scale, but by 1916 only the east wing of the new Hofburg had been built.

This chief official palace of the emperors of Austria ended up as a rather rambling conglomeration of more or less separate royal residences and offices. The buildings range from the great library and the *Augustinerkirche* (where the Habsburgs were buried and where the Vienna Boys' Choir now sings) to the Winter Riding School. The Hofburg was a place of court ceremonial rather than court life. Every year on the Thursday of Passion Week, for example, the *Rittersaal* saw the extraordinary ceremony of the Washing of Feet when the emperor dutifully cleansed the pedal extremities of a dozen elderly male paupers while the empress saw to twelve old ladies: afterwards all 24 were graciously served an elaborate banquet by their royal hosts. The paupers were not actually allowed to eat anything *in situ*; imperial 'take-aways' were supplied for consumption after the paupers had removed themselves from the premises.

The principal living quarters of the Imperial Family at the Hofburg were contained in the Leopold Building and in Fischer von Erlach's Imperial Chancellery. The *piano nobile* or first floor of the former boasts the most sumptuous rooms in the palace, including the ceremonial apartments and the empress's bedroom; whereas the first floor of the Imperial Chancellery accommodated the austere nineteenth-century habits of Franz Joseph. Known to history as the 'first civil servant', Franz Joseph reigned for 68 years (1848–1916) and, especially after the death in 1898 of his wife, the alluring Elisabeth, spent an enormous proportion of those years dedicated to duty at his desk. He preferred to wear the plainest of uniforms and slept in a tiny room furnished with only an iron bedstead and a washstand. The sybaritic Edward VII found visits to the Hofburg a little trying on account of the early dinners, but had to concede his affection for 'that dear old man'.

Like Franz Joseph, Maria Theresa (1717–80) combined majesty with simplicity. The 'Great Empress' was the daughter of Charles VI and inherited the possessions of the Habsburgs in 1740. All subsequent members of the House of Austria descend from Maria Theresa, who married Francis (Franz) of Lorraine. The Habsburg monarchy developed an entirely new character during her reign: she did away with much of the Spanish-style etiquette of the Court of Vienna, while preserving some of the ancient ceremonial, and made herself far more accessible to her subjects than her predecessors had ever been. Born without the dreaded 'Habsburg lip' (an over-large, drooping lower lip), Maria Theresa was very much a German in appearance: a golden-haired pink-and-white Dresden shepherdess when young, a plump and *gemütliche* mother-figure after incessant childbearing had taken away her looks. She also had a typically German bourgeois simplicity. Once, when she made a coffee spot on a State paper she was reading at breakfast, she drew a line round it with her pen and wrote a note of apology.

This very homeliness is a surprising feature of Schönbrunn, the 'Versailles of Austria' on the western outskirts of Vienna, where Maria Theresa took up residence in 1746. Named after the fountain in the park ('*Schöner Brunner*'), Schönbrunn was rebuilt in 1605 as an imperial summer residence after the original fourteenth-century palace was burnt, only to be destroyed by the Turks

39 The Imperial Chancellery (or *Reichskanzlei*) of the 'new' Hofburg, Vienna, which was built by the master of Austrian Imperial Baroque, Johann Bernhard Fischer von Erlach, and his son in the reign of Emperor Charles VI (1711–40).

40 The Spanish Riding School in the Hofburg, Vienna, where the Lipizzaner horses are put through their paces, is another of the Fischer von Erlachs' buildings for Emperor Charles VI in this imperial complex.

when they besieged Vienna in 1683. The second rebuilding from 1696 onwards was Johann Fischer von Erlach's masterpiece, though the architect's first plan was rejected by the Emperor Leopold I as being too grandiose even for a Habsburg of the old school. The glorious yellow façade was given Ionic pilasters between each of the 37 bays, with statues on the balustrade above each pilaster. Inside, the gold and white Great Gallery is impressively Baroque with ceiling frescoes by Gregorio Guglielmi, glittering crystal chandeliers and inlaid wooden floors. The exotically panelled *Millionenzimmer* (or 'Millions Room', so named because it was supposed to have cost a million thalers) featured Indo-Persian miniatures on parchment inlaid into the *boiserie*.

This was all a little too much for the homely Maria Theresa. She employed Nicolaus Pacassi to make Schönbrunn more like a country house than a palace; Fischer von Erlach's three domes over the projecting centre portion of the façade were removed for a start. Then she saw to the relandscaping of the park, adding the botanical gardens, the 'Gloriette' triumphal arch, the obelisk and the Roman ruins. Maria Theresa also added the delightful little Palace Theatre, Baroque outside, Rococo within, where her eleventh daughter Marie Antoinette (later Queen of France) used to perform on the stage. On one occasion, in 1768, Maria Theresa surprised the audience and stopped the actors in their tracks. 'Children', she screamed as she rushed upon the scene, 'Poldi has just had a boy!'

41 (*left*) The Upper Belvedere, Vienna: the entrance façade. Built between 1721 and 1723 by Lukas von Hildebrandt for the military commander, Prince Eugene of Savoy, it was purchased by the Habsburgs in 1752. The artificial lake reflects the colours of the 'garden palace'.

42 (*above*) Maria Theresa's old royal palace at Budapest was probably begun to a plan by Jean-Nicholas Jadot de Ville Issey in 1749 and then completed about 1770 under the supervision of Franz Anton Hildenbrandt. Heavily restored in the nineteenth century, the palace was badly damaged in the siege of 1944–5, since when it has been rebuilt.

Poldi was her third son who became Emperor Leopold II (a bit of a radical whose welcome for the French Revolution lost some of its warmth when his sister went to the guillotine) and the boy in question was the future Franz II who renounced the title of Holy Roman Emperor in 1806 – thus bringing to an end an institution that had lasted for a thousand years.

Maria Theresa and her enormous family brought a jolly domestic warmth to the 1,441 rooms of Schönbrunn during their summer sojourns. Over the last two hundred years many epoch-making events have taken place in the yellow palace. Napoleon resided there in 1805 and 1809, the festivities of the Congress of Vienna took place in 1815 after his defeat; there were also the birth and death of Franz Joseph, the signature of the Act of Renunciation in 1918 by the emperor's successor Karl, the Allied bombing in 1945 – but Maria Theresa's *gemütlich* atmosphere still pervades the place. Such small rooms as the Yellow Drawing Room or Pink Room particularly evoke her cosy spirit.

Maria Theresa was, however, much more than a *Hausfrau*. In addition to carrying out a tremendous programme of administrative and legal reforms, she had to wage a series of wars to defend her inheritance against the claims of Bavaria, Saxony, France and Prussia. At Schönbrunn, Maria Theresa and her Chancellor, Kaunitz, would make their plans. On her accession she first rallied the Austrians to her support with her feminine charm and then set out to reawaken the loyalty of her Hungarian subjects. After her coronation, in accordance with the ancient custom of newly-crowned Hungarian monarchs, she mounted a horse – though she had only just learnt to ride – and galloped up a

43 (*left*) Schönbrunn, Vienna: the garden front. Designed by Fischer von Erlach, and built from 1696 to 1713 for Emperor Leopold I, the yellow palace was later modified by Nicolaus Pacassi for Maria Theresa in 1749.

44 (*below*) The 'Gloriette' triumphal arch in the grounds of Schönbrunn, Vienna, is perhaps better seen from the distance as an eyecatcher. It was erected by Maria Theresa to the designs of Nicolaus Pacassi in celebration of her military victories in the War of the Austrian Succession.

45 (*right*) Schönbrunn, Vienna: the Chinese Room.

46 The mountain eyrie of the sovereign rulers of Liechtenstein in their principality at Vaduz. The medieval *Schloss* was rebuilt in the sixteenth and seventeenth centuries; it passed to the Prince of Liechtenstein in 1712 and has been the permanent residence of the present prince, Franz Joseph, since 1939.

hill, from the top of which she waved her sword to the north, south, east and west over the surrounding plains. As she did so, the crowd cried: 'We will die for our King, Maria Theresa.' Then dressed in black and with St Stephen's crown on her head, she made a moving appeal to the Hungarian Diet, which immediately voted to raise and equip an army for her.

The Hungarian feudal lords so warmed to their young queen that they built her a splendid royal palace in Budapest. Their enthusiasm was not quite matched by their perseverance; for, although the roof was in place in 1752 the castle was not completed until nearly twenty years later. The building seems to have been started to a design by Jean-Nicholas Jadot de Ville Issey in 1749, but the work was later directed from Vienna by the court architect Franz Anton Hildebrandt. In the nineteenth century the royal palace at Budapest was heavily restored, and suffered a terrible fate during the siege of 1944–45, although some careful renovation work has been done.

Maria Theresa's other palace in Hungary, Gödollo, outside Budapest, was designed in the late 1740s by Andreas Mayerhoffer in the Rococo style. Mayerhoffer had been a pupil of Johann Lukas von Hildebrandt who first came to Vienna through service in the army of Prince Eugene of Savoy (1663–1736). It was for this great Imperial Field-Marshal, a junior member of the future ruling dynasty of Italy, that Hildebrandt constructed the creamy confection of the Belvedere in Vienna which was bought by the Habsburgs in 1752.

Prince Eugene's military record was second only to that of the Duke of Marlborough whom he served so well in the War of the Spanish Succession, 1701–14. His triumphs at the head of the Imperial Army included several sound trouncings of the Turks and the storming of Belgrade. As early as 1683 he had earned the undying gratitude of the Habsburgs by driving the Turkish janissaries from the gates of Vienna. Ten years later, he invested in some sloping pasture lands with an eye to his future plan for the Belvedere, the greatest Baroque palace in the Imperial capital.

This 'garden palace' comprises the Lower Belvedere, where Prince Eugene lived in the summer; and, at the top of the terraced garden crisply laid out up the hill, the Upper Belvedere which was used for entertainments. The Lower Belvedere, a sort of Baroque 'bungalow', was built between 1714 and 1716, with an upper floor only in the central part. The Marble Hall inside has a ceiling fresco by Altomonte, depicting Prince Eugene's epic victory in 1716 at Peterwardein, where he defeated a Turkish army twice the size of his own. The same artist was responsible for the ceiling in the Yellow Room where the Prince slept.

The Upper Belvedere, completed in the early 1720s, is a considerably more elaborate affair; indeed it is perhaps a little overdone. The façade has three central sections, two wings and four corner towers for good measure, all of which are reflected in the artificial lake in front of the palace. The interior is a stupendous feast of Baroque decoration, with a double staircase in white marble adorned by cherubs supporting huge wrought-iron lanterns; the central chamber (twice the size of the Marble Hall in the Lower Belvedere) is a riot of red marble and the study is awash with gold leaf. Hildebrandt, the sapper turned architect, let loose a team of Italian artists on the frescoes and wall paintings, and

the results provided endless topics of conversation—or often dumb awe—at Prince Eugene's parties.

The grounds are thick with fountains and statues, and the gardens, all of a piece with the two palaces, complete a gorgeous trinity. The gardens are of both botanical and architectural interest, for Prince Eugene collected rare plants. After his death in 1736, the Belvedere passed to an extravagant female cousin whose excesses led to the garden palace being sold to the family its builder had defended so stoutly.

The Habsburgs' main use for the Belvedere was as an Imperial picture gallery, though it was also useful for entertaining. In April 1770, for instance, there was a memorable court gala here before Marie Antoinette departed to become the bride of Louis XVI. At the end of the nineteenth century, the Archduke Franz Ferdinand (Franz Joseph's nephew and heir presumptive) came to live at the

47 The Lower Belvedere has been called a 'Baroque bungalow', though only the basic structure is single-storeyed. Built from 1714 to 1716 by Lukas von Hildebrandt for Prince Eugene of Savoy, this less elaborate of the two garden palaces was where he actually lived.

48 (*above right*) The Upper Belvedere, Vienna: the Marble Hall, with its rich red marble, gilded wall decoration and parquet floors. Prince Eugene used this palace for entertaining; clearly this is a room (two storeys high) in which to stand rather than to sit.

Belvedere and it was from here that he and his morganatic wife set out on their fateful journey in the early summer of 1914. On 28 June they were assassinated at Sarajevo – bringing the curtain down on Old Europe. At the garden palace of Vienna, a happier event occurred in 1955 when the treaty which restored Austrian independence after the Second World War was signed there.

About the same time as the Belvedere was added to the Habsburg palaces, Maria Theresa began enlarging a country seat at Laxenburg, a few miles south of Vienna. Set in extensive parkland with a lake, Laxenburg lies in the old hunting country of the medieval Dukes of Austria; the Altes Schloss here is said to have been begun in 1381 by Duke Albert III. Maria Theresa wanted something more comfortable for relaxation away from the capital and the attractive two-storey Neues Schloss, built in a mixture of the Baroque and Rococo styles, was well-stocked for diversions, with a theatre and a skittle alley. She also busied herself in the park with the installation of statuary, cascades, temples and the like.

In the early nineteenth century a new Gothic castle was added and around the time of the Congress of Vienna in 1815 Laxenburg became a lively centre of court life. The Congress gave Europe its last spell of stability and in the ensuing years Austria, ruled by the rather colourless Franz II and his abler adviser Metternich, dominated the European scene. Franz and the conservative-minded Metternich, however, erred in not shifting the mentally-deficient heir, Ferdinand, from the line of succession. If they had done so, the revolutionary storms of 1848 might not have shaken the Habsburg Empire as they did. Instead, Ferdinand was allowed to rule as nominal emperor for thirteen years following Franz's death in 1835.

When the upheavals of 1848 brought poor Ferdinand's reign to an end, he was allowed to keep his title of emperor, even though he had abdicated. Ferdinand held his own little court at the royal castle of Prague, where he lived until his death aged 82 in 1875; he was known as '*die Praguer Majestät*' to differentiate him from the reigning emperor (Franz Joseph) in Vienna. Ferdinand had a particular affection for the castle where he had been crowned as King of Bohemia in 1830, the last coronation using the St Wenceslas Crown.

The ancient castle of Prague had been the seat of Czech sovereigns since the ninth century; the Habsburgs acquired the throne in the sixteenth century and extended the castle. At the turn of the seventeenth century Prague knew the splendour of Rudolf II's Imperial court, and the castle benefited from the attentions of fine craftsmen; but the Czech revolt brought that to an end. Further damage to the castle was done in the Prussian Siege in 1757 and the renovation work was carried out by the Viennese architect Pacassi (who also worked at Schönbrunn). But until Ferdinand's arrival the Habsburgs tended only to come here for coronations and the occasional brief visit.

The long years of exile were brightened for Ferdinand by his daily stroll along the ramparts of Prague Castle where he would receive the respectful salutes of the citizens. He was conscious of his Imperial birthright and when denied his favourite fare protested vigorously: 'I *am* the Emperor and I *will* have dumplings!'

Ferdinand's nephew Franz Joseph was a fairly frequent visitor to another Habsburg palace, the imperial castle of Salzburg, which came to the dynasty early in the nineteenth century after many years as an archiepiscopal residence. It was here in 1867 that Franz Joseph entertained Napoleon III and, four years later, the newly proclaimed German Emperor, Wilhelm I.

After his defeat by Prussia in 1866 Franz Joseph came to realize that the sphere of influence of the Habsburg monarchy lay not in Germany but eastward along the Danube, as a bulwark against Russia and a refuge for the smaller nations of Central Europe. In the end it was only Franz Joseph's will and the power of his name which kept the ramshackle Empire together: Karl I reigned only two years (1916–18) before being deposed.

Today Liechtenstein is the only surviving monarchy in the whole of Central Europe. The state takes its name from its rulers, and consists of two former fiefs of the Holy Roman Empire, Schellenberg and Vaduz, which in 1699 and 1712 were bought from the impoverished Count Jakob Hannibal III of Hohenems by Prince Johann Adam of Liechtenstein, the head of a wealthy Austrian noble family unconnected with the territory that was soon to bear his name. As the owner of these fiefs, Johann Adam was admitted to the Imperial College of Princes; and in 1719, his cousin and successor, Anton Florian, was recognized as a sovereign by the Emperor Charles VI to whom he had been tutor, his two fiefs being erected into a hereditary state of the Holy Roman Empire under the name of the Principality of Liechtenstein.

Johann Adam did not acquire his two fiefs out of any desire to rule, but simply in order to give his House the prestige of being sovereign princes. And indeed, until 1842, the princes of Liechtenstein never set foot in their little Alpine principality, but continued to live as great nobles on their estates in Austria and

49 Prague Castle (the *Hradčany*), which was the official seat and place of coronation of Czech sovereigns from the end of the nineteenth century up to 1918. Its present appearance is largely due to the renovations by Nicolaus Pacassi after the Prussian siege in 1757.

50 (*right*) The Imperial Castle at Salzburg, adjoining the cathedral, came into the possession of the Habsburgs in 1816, having previously been an archiepiscopal residence. Rebuilt in the early seventeenth century by Archbishop Wolf Dietrich, it was enlarged about 1780.

Bohemia and in their palaces in Vienna, where their world-famous art collections were housed.

The Liechtensteins, in turn, took their name from the Castle of Liechtenstein, not far from Laxenburg outside Vienna, where the founder of the House, Hugo, lived in the twelfth century. Both their palaces in Vienna, the *Gartenpalais* and the *Stadtpalais*, were designed by Martinelle around the turn of the eighteenth century when the dynasty was waxing. The *Gartenpalais* is a vast High Baroque affair, completed in 1711, with a plain façade and five arched doorways. The Garden Room is notable for its paired Tuscan columns, and the Marble Hall for its chimney-pieces and pedestals, and columns of red marble with gilded capitals and a ceiling by Pozzo. Outside, the landscaped park has an English air, though it was originally laid out in the French manner.

The Liechtenstein *Stadtpalais* was completed by de Gabrieli who made some changes to the original design by Martinelle. The doorways are of outstanding

51 (*above left*) Schönbrunn *en fête* for the Diamond Jubilee celebrations of Emperor Franz Joseph in 1908. Born here in 1830, the emperor lived at Schönbrunn in austere style until his death in 1916. After a 68-year reign many of his subjects had come to believe that the venerable, white-whiskered Emperor was immortal.

52 (*above centre*) Vaduz Schloss: a dining-room in the seat of the Princes of Liechtenstein. The family is famous for its great art collection; here fine furniture and tapestries are displayed.

53 (*above right*) The Castle of Liechtenstein: the medieval stronghold in Lower Austria from which the family derives its name. It was acquired by Hugo of Liechtenstein in the twelfth century on account of its strategic importance.

quality: the main entrance boasts rich sculptural decoration and the side door (dated 1705) has Atlas figures on high plinths. Above the centre of the entrance façade, with its Corinthian pilasters, is a gallery-like attic decorated with figures. The interior of the *Stadtpalais* is magnificently Rococo; one of the fine suite of reception rooms has a chimney-piece by Canova.

The Liechtenstein dynasty distinguished themselves in the Imperial Army and as patrons of the arts. Joseph Wenzel, one of Maria Theresa's field-marshals in the Seven Years' War, was an enthusiastic collector as was his great-nephew, Aloys I, during whose long reign as Prince of Liechtenstein the dynasty became the richest family in the Empire. Aloys's brother and successor, Johann I, was another great soldier like Joseph Wenzel, eventually succeeding to the command of the Imperial forces.

It was Aloys II, Johann's son, who made history by being the first sovereign of Liechtenstein to visit his principality. Johann II, another patron of the arts, known as 'The Good', reigned for more than 70 years from 1858. The upheavals of those years, which drove so many other dynasties out of their kingdoms, only served to tie the family and the principality more closely together. The break-up of the Habsburg Empire saw Liechtenstein still independent and still under the sovereignty of its venerable and much-loved prince. The only change was that the Principality unhitched itself from the Austrian economy and joined that of Switzerland. At the same time, Johann II lost most of his vast family seats in Bohemia (now Czechoslovakia), which meant that his successors looked increasingly towards the Principality. By the end of the Second World War, Liechtenstein had become the real home of its Prince, Franz Joseph II; and the famed Liechtenstein pictures had been moved from Vienna to their mountain stronghold at Vaduz.

The origins of Vaduz Castle probably date back to the twelfth century, while the rocky ledge on which it stands is said to have been inhabited as early as the Bronze Age. The walls of the old tower are up to 12 feet thick in places and those of the north-east round tower, added in the sixteenth century, are even thicker. The exterior of Vaduz has been described as resembling a cross between a medieval fortress and a granary. The interior was completely restored by Johann the Good and has recently been stylishly redesigned for Prince Franz Joseph. There are well over 100 rooms at Vaduz but even they do not provide enough space to display all of the prince's fabulous art collection. Put together over several centuries, the collection is a major interest of Prince Franz Joseph's and it is said that, under different circumstances, he would have liked to be a professor of art history.

The people of the little principality remain devoted to the dynasty, under whose rule they enjoy a happy and prosperous existence which the inhabitants of the larger European states might well envy. Liechtenstein's main source of income today comes from providing anonymity and tax-havens for the super-rich and for mighty corporations. Of the European sovereigns reigning at the present time, Prince Franz Joseph, whose mother was a daughter of the Archduke Karl Ludwig, has most Habsburg blood.

The German Kingdoms

PRUSSIA, BAVARIA, HANOVER, SAXONY AND WÜRTTEMBERG

54 (*previous page*) Schleissheim, north of Munich. The central three-storeyed block was designed by Enrico Zuccalli who remodelled the palace from 1684; the rest, the work of Joseph Effner, was executed at various stages between 1701 and 1727. Carbonet and Girard, the landscapers of Nymphenburg and pupils of Le Nôtre, laid out the French-style gardens. (*See page 87*)

55 (*below*) The Berlin *Schloss* was razed to the ground by the Russians in 1950 after being slightly damaged by bombing five years earlier. It was the finest work of Andreas Schlüter; the south façade (shown here) was built in a sculptured Roman Baroque style (1698–1706).

The proclamation of William I as German Emperor at Versailles in 1871, after the Franco-Prussian War, was the climax of Bismarck's plan to create a united Germany with the Prussian House of Hohenzollern at its head. There was something especially appropriate in the Iron Chancellor's choice of Versailles for this Prussian apotheosis as the first Prussian king, Frederick I (crowned in 1701), had tried to model himself on Louis XIV, even arranging his day in accordance with the timetable at Versailles.

Thanks to the achievement of Frederick's father, Frederick William (the 'Great Elector' of Brandenburg), the Hohenzollerns were, by the end of the seventeenth century, among the more important of the many royal and ducal families ruling over a wide assortment of German states. The ambitious Frederick induced the Emperor (Charles VI) to recognize him as a king in return for promising his support in the War of the Spanish Succession (1701–14). He had to take his kingly title from outside the Holy Roman Empire and so he became King of Prussia, an outlying province of his to the east of Brandenburg, from which it was separated by Polish territory. Later, the name of Prussia came to be applied to Brandenburg itself and to other dominions of the Hohenzollern kings; and the original province of that name became known as East Prussia.

Having become a king, Frederick I embraced with enthusiasm the notion of monarchical splendour. He even took a mistress so as to be like *Le Grand Monarque*, though he much preferred his second wife, who was a sister of George I of Great Britain. To provide a suitable background to his newly-won majesty he built three great palaces: the Berlin Schloss, Charlottenburg and the town palace at Potsdam.

The Berlin Schloss, a bold Roman Baroque effort built from 1698 to 1716 by the sculptor-architect Andreas Schlüter, was damaged by Allied bombs in 1945. Although the damage was in fact only slight, the Schloss was razed to the ground by the Russians five years later to create the Marx-Engels Platz in East Berlin. Sir Sacheverell Sitwell, that masterly observer of the Baroque, found the palace 'most hideous of its race'. The façades were 'very ugly', while the two great saloons with stucco decorations by Schlüter showed, in Sir Sacheverell's view, the eighteenth century 'in nefarious competition with our own for the prize of clumsy ugliness'.

Charlottenburg was named after Frederick I's second wife Sophie Charlotte, the 'philosopher queen' and friend of Leibnitz, who died in 1705. It had been begun ten years earlier as a smallish country house, called Lutzenburg, by Arnold Nering and was then enlarged by the court architect, a Swede called Johann Eosander who was later ennobled as 'von Goethe'. An oversized cupola, topped by a gilded figure of Fortune blowing in the wind, dominates the palace. Eosander von Goethe was very much under the influence of Versailles, and added an orangery after visiting the palace of *Le Roi Soleil*.

In the time of Frederick I's grandson, Frederick II (the Great), Charlottenburg was revamped by his friend Georg von Knobelsdorff, a Prussian aristocrat who had abandoned a military career for the arts. He added the east wing with its suite of exquisite Rococo rooms, notably the *Goldene Galerie*, decorated by the sculptor Johann August Nahl. Further additions and

56 (*bottom*) The staircase of the Berlin *Schloss*. The sculpture in the palace survived the bombing of 1945 and was apparently removed before the Russians blew the building up.

57 (*below*) Charlottenburg: the entrance front. Begun by Arnold Nering in 1695, the palace was completed to the designs of the Swedish architect Eosander von Goethe in 1712. An east wing was added by Georg von Knobelsdorff in the 1740s. The gilded figure of Fortuna on the top of the outsize cupola acts as a weather-vane. Charlottenburg has been carefully restored since the war. Andreas Schlüter's statue of the Great Elector, which used to stand in front of the Berlin *Schloss*, was moved here at the end of the Second World War.

alterations were made later in the eighteenth and early nineteenth centuries, including the mausoleum in the grounds by Karl Friedrich Schinkel.

Like so many German palaces, Charlottenburg suffered badly in the Second World War. In a single air raid in November 1943 the central block and the Knobelsdorff wing were burnt out and the entire palace seriously damaged – in some cases, such as the theatre and the Belvedere, beyond repair. However, much restoration has been carried out. In an imaginative gesture the bronze equestrian statue of the Great Elector by Schlüter, which used to stand outside the Berlin Schloss, was moved into the forecourt at Charlottenburg. Inside, with the help of photographs fortuitously taken just before the Allied bombs were dropped, laborious efforts have been made to recreate the rooms as they were in the days of Frederick the Great and his grandfather. A special feature of the former's apartments is the French collection of pictures, particularly Watteau's shop sign for the merchant jeweller Gersaint of Notre-Dame bridge, painted in 1720 and purchased by the Prussian king thirty years later. To Frederick the Great, France was the last word in civilization.

Rather unprepossessing in appearance, with large and brilliant blue eyes gazing out of a thin pale face, Frederick the Great was artistic and intellectual to a degree that infuriated his boorish father, Frederick William I (a victim of the dread 'royal disease' porphyria). On one notorious occasion, after the young Frederick had tried in vain to run away, his best friend was beheaded in his presence by order of his father. Having become king at the age of 28 in 1740, Frederick was able to indulge in all the things which he most enjoyed, and which his father had most despised: poetry, flute-playing, witty conversation, building palaces and collecting works of art.

In 1744 Frederick gave his friend Knobelsdorff the job of rebuilding Frederick I's *Stadtschloss* (town palace) at Potsdam, just outside Berlin. The result was both monumental and beautiful, with Corinthian colonnades projecting from the façades. Inside, the silvered *boiseries* so characteristic of the 'Frederick Rococo' style were much in evidence. Although his architect fitted in an imperial staircase by enlarging the central pavilion, Frederick, who was susceptible to draughts, did not care for great Baroque staircases and insisted upon a special smaller flight leading to his private apartments. Sadly, the

58 The now vanished Town Palace (*Stadtschloss*), Potsdam: the entrance front. Knobelsdorff rebuilt Frederick I's old structure in 1744, though he retained Jean de Bodt's Fortuna Portal. The Town Palace was destroyed in the Second World War.

Stadtschloss of Potsdam is no more, having been destroyed, together with most of the centre of the town, in the Second World War.

Frederick the Great's differences of opinion with Knobelsdorff reached breaking-point over the more intimate palace of Sans Souci set in parkland about a mile away from the *Stadtschloss*. Frederick wanted a single-storey structure, without a basement, at the top of a hill terraced with vineyards; Knobelsdorff argued in favour of a cellar floor, on account of the dampness of the sand underneath, and of raising the palace on a plinth so as to be seen from the bottom of the terraces. The patron had the last word and the architect was eventually sacked. Frederick was adamant in his desire to walk out of his windows straight into the garden, but there is no doubt that Knobelsdorff was right on both counts. Seen from below, the little pink and white palace does not stand high enough above the six terraces, seeming as if it is cut in half. The Prussian climate was, of course, not suited to vines so Frederick had them enclosed in a dozen glasshouses which were soon given over to other exotic fruit and flowers.

Above the portico of the dining-room, the king had inscribed the words SANS SOUCI to capture the carefree spirit of the summer palace. The interior remains the finest example of its kind: the Corinthian and cupola halls, the latter with a marble intarsia floor; the music-room with wall paintings by the court painter Antoine Pesne (a Frenchman, needless to say); the yellow Flower Room. Sans

59 Sans Souci, Potsdam: the garden front, with the name above the door like any suburban home. This was the favourite residence of Frederick the Great, who moved here in May 1747 when it was completed by Knobelsdorff. The flawed design, whereby the palace appears to be bisected by the terrace, was the fault of the king rather than the architect. The greenhouses were Frederick's attempt to cheat nature.

Souci was ready for occupation in May 1747 and Frederick wasted no time in moving into what was to become his favourite residence. There was not a German volume to be found on the shelves of the little circular library, while the picture gallery was hung with French favourites such as Watteau and Lancret. The king's bedroom, more Classical than Rococo with its Ionic columns, was decorated in pastel shades. There the visitor can see his magnificent French eighteenth-century writing table and the winged chair in which he died in 1786.

After the Seven Years' War against Austria, Russia and France, which ended in 1763 with his victory, Frederick indulged himself once more in an orgy of building, adding the extravagant Neues Palais to the ensemble at Potsdam. As this colossal pile was situated only about a mile to the west of his beloved Sans Souci it was not clear to his somewhat disgruntled subjects why the king felt the need for yet another palace. Some people considered he built the Neues Palais to show the world he was not ruined by the war; others that it was meant to be a shop-front for Prussian goods (an important role for a royal palace, as Colbert discovered at Versailles). In any event, Frederick appeared to take little interest in the designs by the architect Johann Buring, under whose supervision the palace was built from 1763 to 1769. The whole exercise cost about half a million pounds.

Frederick described the Neues Palais as a *Fanfaronade* (a piece of ostentation); it certainly conveys a theatrical sense of power. The massive exterior is red brick, rather Dutch in manner; on the roof, the king cocked a snook at his opponents in the Seven Years' War – bearing a closed crown are the naked figures of the Empress, the Tsarina and Madame de Pompadour. Inside, the emphasis is on display, with a 100-foot-long marble concert-hall and a theatre for 500 people.

60 (*above left*) The *Neues Palais*, Potsdam. Frederick the Great's expensive 'grand gesture' was built between 1763 and 1769 to the designs of Johann Büring. The wives or mistresses of the king's enemies are among the naked figures on the roof.

61 (*above centre*) The luminescent Chinese Pavilion, in the pleasure grounds of Potsdam, was built for Frederick the Great by Büring between 1754 and 1756. The portico on each front has two conversation pieces: one is a tea ceremony, the other is of young ladies being offered exotic fruits. The figures are by Benkerl and Heymüller. The eight columns (four to each portico) are actually gilded palm trees.

62 (*above right*) Sans Souci: the Marble Hall
designed by Knobelsdorff, with a floor
designed by Johann Christian Hoppenhaupt and
executed in marble intarsia by Duquesnoy. The
Italian marble blocks were worked 'in the rough'
at Hamburg by Heller and Grepler.

Here the king would come on formal occasions with visiting sovereigns and
other grand guests. The interior decoration of the Neues Palais puts it in a class
apart. Sir Sacheverell Sitwell considers that

> there are two floors, in which the French art of the period at its highest
> expression can be seen to absolute perfection. The boiseried rooms
> decorated in silver are quite inconceivable in their loveliness; many of the
> doors have a wave-like waterfall treatment which is again echoed in some of
> the wall-panels in two shades of gold, or with a greenish silver that gives
> variety to that more conventional shade of moonlight. The rooms are full of
> superb furniture of the date, and pictures by Watteau can surely have never
> found a more congenial environment.

After Frederick the Great's death, Prussia entered a period of stagnation leading
to the indignities of the Napoleonic Wars; but then another period of
regeneration followed until Frederick William IV's exaggerated view of his
royal power was checked in 1848. One of the consequences of the upheavals in
that 'year of revolutions' was a move to create a German Empire with the King
of Prussia as Emperor. However, the strongly legitimist Frederick William
refused the Imperial crown, later accepted by his brother William.

Frederick William IV rebuilt Schloss Stolzenfels, south of Koblenz, to the designs of Schinkel from 1836 to 1842. Towering over the Rhine, this crenellated neo-Gothic castle is a sort of Teutonic cross between an English and a Spanish country seat. The unfortunate Frederick William, who had leanings towards scholarship and the natural sciences, became mentally deranged following a stroke in 1857. William took over as Regent, duly succeeding to the throne on his brother's death in 1861. Stolzenfels is now a museum.

Among the various other residences occupied by the German Imperial family were Friedrichshof, Cecilienhof and Marmorpalais. The first-named was the home of the Empress Frederick, Queen Victoria's eldest daughter, whose husband reigned for only 98 days after he eventually succeeded William I in 1888. The Empress antagonized the Prussians by her tactless, even aggressive, Englishness. It was not just that she complained of the stiffness of the Prussian court etiquette and the shortage of bathrooms in the Berlin Schloss; she would persist in speaking of England as 'home'.

When her son, the Kaiser William II (who liked to blame his dislocated neck and withered arm on the English obstetrician who probably saved his life),

63 The Empress Frederick, dressed in widow's weeds, with her family at Friedrichshof, in the Taunus Hills, in 1897. On her right are her sons-in-law, the future King Constantine I of Greece, Prince Adolf of Schaumburg-Lippe and Prince Friedrich Karl of Hesse; on her left are her daughter Princess Margarete of Prussia, her nephew Prince Albert of Schleswig-Holstein and two more daughters, the future Queen Sophie of Greece and Princess Viktoria of Prussia. In front of the Empress Frederick are her grandchildren (from left to right): Prince Maximilian of Hesse, Prince Friedrich Wilhelm of Hesse, the future King George II of Greece, the future King Alexander I of Greece (who was mortally poisoned by a monkey) and the future Queen Helen of Roumania (who died in 1982). What the English-minded Empress Frederick, Queen Victoria's eldest daughter, had in mind when she built Friedrichshof was something along the lines of Osborne.

64 The Residenz, Munich, developed over several centuries to a palatial size with seven inner courtyards. This is the octagonal *Brunnenhof* (or Fountain Court), which derives its name from the early-seventeenth-century fountain in the middle.

offered the Empress Frederick a grace-and-favour residence for her widowhood she refused. Instead she decided to build a country house in the English style on a 250-acre estate at Kronberg near the Rhine in the forests of the Taunus Hills. The idea she had in mind for Friedrichshof was something along the lines of Osborne; the German architect was told that nothing about it should catch the eye, but that it should hold the gaze. She wanted somewhere to house her art collection and, especially, her papers; Queen Victoria and her eldest daughter ('The Other Victoria') carried on a voluminous correspondence. In one of her letters to the matriarch of Europe, the Empress Frederick described Friedrichshof as nothing extraordinary, but solid and in good taste. An amalgam of Tudor, Italian Renaissance and eighteenth-century Classical, the house was comfortable without appearing too grand. The Empress Frederick was particularly proud of the park she had reclaimed from the forest, and enjoyed strolling in the rose-garden she had planted.

Marmorpalais and Cecilienhof are both in Potsdam. The latter was the home of the Kaiser's son, 'Little Willy' (described by Consuelo Vanderbilt as having 'a silly expression that accentuated the degeneracy of his appearance'), and later had a place in history when the Potsdam Agreement was signed there by Churchill, Stalin and Truman in 1945.

The German Empire had, of course, come to an end following the First World War when the Kaiser abdicated as German Emperor and King of Prussia. In his own way the Kaiser had dominated the European scene more than any other Hohenzollern (with the possible exception of Frederick the Great), a brisk, breezy, slightly flashy figure, moustache erect and uniform resplendent. Today

65 The 'Disneyland' castle of Neuschwanstein,
which was Ludwig II of Bavaria's first major
building scheme. Designed by Eduard Riedel,
Georg Dollmann and Julius Hofmann, the
Wagnerian fairy-tale structure was erected
between 1869 and 1892, but never completed.

66 Nymphenburg, Munich. Still the seat of the Wittelsbach dynasty, this palace was formerly their summer residence. It was built from the mid-seventeenth to the mid-eighteenth century. The Elector Max Emmanuel added four pavilions linked by arcaded galleries to the central edifice. His successors, Karl Albrecht and Maximilian III Josef, continued the Versailles style by constructing the outbuildings in a semi-circle. The park and gardens were laid out from 1701.

the present head of the House of Prussia, 'Little Willy's' son, lives a rather more modest existence in a bungalow on the outskirts of Berlin.

The head of the Wittelsbach House of Bavaria, Prince Albrecht, Duke of Bavaria, still has his seat at Nymphenburg, the Baroque palace outside Munich. Although the Wittelsbachs lost the throne of Bavaria during a Communist uprising in 1918, they are the dynasty which, out of all the former ruling families of Europe, has retained most of its former standing. Historically, the dynasty ranks second only to the Habsburgs among the German Catholic houses.

No less a personage than Charlemagne has the place of honour in the gallery of Wittelsbach ancestors at the Munich Residenz, the palace in the town where the family have been based since the Middle Ages. An irregular complex of buildings, the Residenz consists of seven courtyards built at an angle to the earliest surviving part, the Antiquarium in the south-east corner. This was built in the Italian Renaissance style in 1570 in order to house Albrecht V's collection of Classical antiquities. The Residenz was added to at various times; for instance, the Kaiserhof buildings and the *Residenzstrasse* façade date from the early seventeenth century, whereas the neo-Classical structures of the *Festsaalbau* and the *Königsbau* by Leo von Klenze are early nineteenth century.

The chief delights of the Residenz are the surviving works by François Cuvilliés, the dwarf Walloon master of the Rococo, who began life as a page to the Elector Max Emmanuel in 1708. The stucco decoration of the State Rooms benefited from his lightness of touch and in the Porcelain Rooms (designed to

show off pieces from Meissen, Nymphenburg and Sèvres) there is fine furniture made by Miroffsky to the designs of Cuvilliés. His Rococo masterpiece at the Residenz, though, is the theatre, with its four tiers of boxes, which was built in the 1750s. Here in 1781, *Idomeneo* was produced for the first time; no one could imagine a better setting for a Mozart opera. As Sir Sacheverell Sitwell has said, 'the whole affair looks as though it would fade away and dissolve with the end of each air'. In Sir Sacheverell's view this is the 'absolute culmination' of Rococo art; those seeking the definition of the difference between the terms 'Baroque' and 'Rococo' are advised to compare this theatre with the slightly earlier (1748) opera-house at Bayreuth, still in use as a balance to Wagner's Festival Theatre.

The Residenz was badly damaged in the Second World War, but the interiors—many of which were stripped and stored away for the duration of the conflict—have been painstakingly reconstructed so that it has retained its reputation as a major showplace. The treasury, one of the most important in Europe, includes a small Renaissance statue of St George and the Dragon adorned with 2,291 diamonds, 209 pearls and 406 rubies.

67 (*above left*) Nymphenburg, Munich: the Hunting Room in the exquisite Amalienburg Pavilion. The pavilion, which is regarded as the *ne plus ultra* of Rococo decoration, was built as a hunting-lodge for the Electress Amalia from 1734 to 1739 by François Cuvilliés. In this room devoted to the pleasures of the chase there are pictures by P. Horemans and others. The wall-clock over the fireplace is of Japanese porcelain with Dresden china flowers.

68 (*above centre*) The Hall of Mirrors in the Amalienburg Pavilion, Nymphenburg. As well as Cuvilliés, others involved included J. B. Zimmermann (stucco), J. Dietrich (woodcarving), P. Moretti (decorative painting), and, in all probability, the elder E. Verhelst and J. Gerstens. The style of the latter Dutch sculptor and decorator can be detected in the silver-gilt console tables in this Hall.

69 (*above right*) Nymphenburg: the south-west corner of the Great Hall. The part of the hall overlooking the garden was divided into two storeys by François Cuvilliés in 1756–7 and the superb late-Rococo decoration by J. B. Zimmermann (then aged 76) and his son Franz dates from the same time. The hall has been used for banquets and for concerts. The ceiling painting (*top right*) depicts the goddess Flora receiving the homage of her nymphs.

The Electors of Bavaria used to travel by barge down the canal to their summer palace of Nymphenburg, which was originated in 1664. The Elector Max Emmanuel (whose Savoyard mother had built the five-storey block to the designs of Agostino Borelli) later added four pavilions which were linked by arcaded galleries to the central edifice. His successors took up these echoes of Versailles by constructing a semi-circle of outbuildings. Inside, the features of Nymphenburg include the Banqueting-Hall with its Rococo stuccowork and frescoes by the Zimmermanns; and, in the south pavilion, the Gallery of Beauties painted by Stieler for King Ludwig I.

The most delightful aspect of Nymphenburg, however, lies in its park which was enlarged by Carbonet and Girard, pupils of Le Nôtre, at the beginning of the eighteenth century. Near the Grand Canal were added four more exquisite pavilions: the Pagodenburg, Badenburg, Magdalenklause and, above all else, the Amalienburg. The latter appears to be a simple hunting-lodge consisting of lobbies, a saloon, a bedroom, and a Dutch-tiled kitchen, but the decoration by Cuvilliés makes this one of the most supreme examples of Rococo art. The

70 (*left*) The Singers' Hall, with its coffered ceiling, occupies almost the whole of the fourth floor of Neuschwanstein. The architect, Julius Hofmann, was clearly inspired by Wartburg castle, the Thuringian fortress where the legendary poetical contest is said to have taken place in the thirteenth century. Wagner immortalized this scene in his opera *Tannhäuser*.

71 (*right*) Schleissheim, near Munich: the staircase. Effner called in the great plasterer J. B. Zimmermann to do the complete stuccowork here in the early 1720s. At that time the stairs were of wood; they were faced in marble in the nineteenth century.

bedroom is lavishly decorated in gold; the breathtaking beauty of the saloon comes from an intricate network of silver stucco and woodwork reflected in an octagon of mirrors.

The French pair of Carbonet and Girard also laid out the formal gardens at another Electoral retreat only a barge-journey away from Munich, Schleissheim. Max Emmanuel, who badly wished to copy Versailles, sent Enrico Zuccalli to Paris to absorb some of the atmosphere into his designs for the aggrandisement of Schleissheim, but the architect seemed more interested in copying Bernini. Progress was not nearly fast enough for the Elector and by the early 1700s Zuccalli had completed only one of the four planned wings. Thanks to some slapdash work, the result of pressure to keep the Elector's schedules, parts of the interior promptly collapsed. Max Emmanuel later brought in his gardener's son Joseph Effner to complete the job. The result is a monumental example of German Baroque, with a grand staircase decorated by Johann Zimmermann.

In 1805, having shrewdly thrown in his lot with Napoleon, the Elector Maximilian was able to assume the title of King of Bavaria and add to his territories. Later, before the Battle of Leipzig, Maximilian I prudently changed over to the Allied side, consolidating his position at the peace. Thus Bavaria was established as the most powerful German kingdom after Prussia.

Maximilian's son, Ludwig I, had all the traditional Wittelsbach characteristics: the love of art and architecture, the romantic spirit, the erratic and contradictory temperament. He was both wise and irresponsible; he jealously guarded his royal prerogative, yet was democratically minded and would walk unattended about the streets of Munich. He shocked his conservative and devoutly Catholic subjects by visiting Goethe. While spending millions on putting up magnificent Classical buildings in Munich and elsewhere in his kingdom, he was tight-fisted in his personal expenditure; his clothes were threadbare, and it was said that he would refuse to have onions at the Residenz because they cost too much. Though he was a devoted husband and father, he could not resist a pretty face. This proved his undoing when, in 1846, shortly after his sixtieth birthday, he fell under the spell of the dancer and adventuress Lola Montez. In 1848 there were riots in Munich which led to his abdication.

Ludwig's eldest son and successor, Maximilian II (r. 1848–64), was the least typical of the nineteenth-century Wittelsbachs, except that, like other members of his family, he was something of a scholar and enjoyed intellectual society. Both in character and appearance he resembled his contemporary, Prince Albert, the consort of Queen Victoria. At Hohenschwangau, a castle in the mountains of Upper Bavaria which he rebuilt in 'gingerbread' Gothic, he created a Bavarian Balmoral. When Maximilian bought the place in 1832 it was the ruin of a medieval stronghold, but from 1833 to 1838 he reconstructed it to the designs of Domenico Quaglio, a painter and stage designer. The swans on the lakes below, which provided an heraldic link between the medieval lords of Schwangau and the legendary Swan-Knight Lohengrin, were taken up as a motif for the interior decoration. The walls were smothered with frescoes of medieval chronicles by Moritz von Schwind. A lighter note was struck by the charming cherry and maplewood Biedermeier furniture.

As well as rebuilding Hohenschwangau, Maximilian II also completely renovated a royal 'toy castle', Schloss Berg on Lake Starnberg, with the help of Edward Riedel. Berg was just across the water from the country retreat of the head of the junior branch of the family, Duke Max in Bavaria, whose daughters Elisabeth (the future Empress of Austria) and Sophie were the only women to play any real part in the saga of Ludwig II: Elisabeth was his confidante, Sophie briefly his *fiancée*.

Again like Prince Albert, Maximilian II died young, a martyr to his sense of duty. Although in poor health he insisted on returning to Munich from Italy (where he had repaired to escape the rigours of the Bavarian winter) at the time of the Schleswig-Holstein crisis in 1864. His son, Ludwig II, thus became king at the early age of nineteen. He was a romantically beautiful young man: tall, with delicately chiselled features, blue eyes full of fire and dark, wavy hair. To his subjects, he seemed like Apollo or Prince Charming come to life. 'Now we have

72 Hohenschwangau: the Bavarian Balmoral rebuilt by Maximilian II between 1832 and 1836 to the designs of Domenico Quaglio, a painter and stage designer.

an angel on the throne', drooled the court archivist, though his ministers found him obstinate and difficult to control. He was, however, highly intelligent and at first threw himself wholeheartedly into the affairs of state, for which he had little inclination. His mind was far above such matters. 'This man has something great and poetic about him', wrote Maria de la Paz, Infanta of Spain, 'and has powers of imagination such as one rarely finds in anyone.'

Ever since he had first heard *Lohengrin* at the age of sixteen, the 'Dream King' had been enraptured by the operas of Richard Wagner. Wagner had written, in his preface to the published *Ring* poem, that it would be impossible to achieve the costly productions to which he aspired without the patronage of a German prince. Ludwig had read these words and was determined that this prince should be himself. A month after his accession, he sent his photograph, a ring and an offer of help to Wagner, whose fortunes were then at their lowest ebb.

Thus began the celebrated friendship between the king and the composer, which lasted until Wagner's death. Thanks to Ludwig's patronage, Wagner was able to complete the four operas of the *Ring* cycle and *Parsifal*, and to produce *Tristan*, hitherto regarded as unproducible. Posterity therefore owes Ludwig an immeasurable debt.

At the time, however, Ludwig's subjects thought only of the vast sums of money which were being put at Wagner's disposal. They viewed his ascendancy over the king with misgivings, comparing him to Lola Montez and nicknaming him 'Lolus'. As Wagner said of Ludwig: 'He is, alas, so beautiful, spiritual, soulful and splendid that I fear his life must run away like a fleeting heavenly dream in this common world.'

The fact that the chief opposition to Wagner came from the people of Munich increased Ludwig's dislike for his capital; he took to spending most of his time at Hohenschwangau, in the Swan Country, steeped in the legend of Lohengrin. Wagner would play to him on the maplewood piano in the Hohenstaufen Room. With Ludwig's dislike for Munich went a dislike for appearing in public. When in 1875, he held a review of his troops, it was the first time that the people of his capital had seen him for many years. They were aghast at how he had changed. He was now bearded, and over-indulgence had made him portly and middle-aged, though he was only thirty. Four years earlier, without leaving the seclusion of his mountain retreat, Ludwig had made his sole appearance on the stage of European politics, when, at Bismarck's instigation, he wrote his famous letter inviting King William of Prussia to become German Emperor. In return, Bavaria was granted special privileges within the new Reich; and the Wittelsbachs were promised the reversion of the Imperial Crown in the unlikely event of the Hohenzollerns becoming extinct.

It was mainly on account of his extravagance in building palaces that Ludwig's ministers decided to have him certified as insane. There was his Wagnerian fairy-tale castle of Neuschwanstein, on the mountainside above Hohenschwangau; there was Linderhof, his charming, sugary '*Petit Trianon*'; most costly of all, there was Herrenchiemsee, a replica of the middle part of Versailles, complete with a *Galerie des Glaces*, built on an island in Bavaria's largest lake. The last two were inspired by Ludwig's passion for Marie

Antoinette (godmother to Ludwig I) and for Louis XIV, which existed alongside his devotion to the Wagnerian epics.

The Dream King's mania for building first took practical shape in the Winter Garden on the roof of his apartment at the Munich Residenz in 1867; an iron and glass construction, later extended, it evoked an exotic scene complete with a boat on a lake, jungle vegetation, an Oriental kiosk and a backdrop of the Himalayas. At the same time, he redecorated his rooms at the Residenz in a Louis XIV style with the help of a theatre designer, Franz Seitz.

The pinnacled and turreted Neuschwanstein had a long building history which stretched to 1892, half-a-dozen years after Ludwig II's death; even then it was never completed as the projected chapel was abandoned. Three architects were involved: Eduard Riedel (1869–74), who had worked on Berg; Georg Dollmann (1874–84), the son-in-law of Ludwig I's architect Leo von Klenze; and Julius Hofmann (1884–92). The latter was responsible for most of the interiors, though their decoration varies from the late Gothic of the king's bedroom to the Byzantine of the Throne Room. The vast Singers' Hall is reminiscent of the Wartburg Castle where Tannhäuser's poetical contest took place; the winter garden next to the artificial stalactite grotto also recalls this Wagnerian legend. Ludwig II saw Neuschwanstein as reflecting 'the true style of the ancient German knights' castles'. He would watch its progress from a telescope in his bedroom at Hohenschwangau, but was to spend only about 100 days there.

73 (*above*) Ludwig II's bedroom at Neuschwanstein was among the first interiors to be completed in the castle in the 1880s. The style is Teutonically late-Gothic; the architect Julius Hofmann based the design on a painting by Peter Herwegen executed in 1869. Above the carved walnut bed (in which the king spent remarkably little time) there is a 'perfect forest of tiny Gothic spires'. It is said that the *boiseries* of this room kept 17 woodcarvers busy for nearly five years.

74 (*right*) The Peacock Throne, in the middle of the Moorish Kiosk at Linderhof, was designed by Franz Seitz and made for Ludwig II in Paris by Le Blanc Granger in 1876.

Ludwig II's favourite residence was Linderhof, set in a delightful park underneath the forests of the Ammergau Alps. Georg Dollmann transformed an old hunting-lodge of Maximilian II into a royal villa with a Baroque façade and Rococo interiors from 1874 to 1879. The decoration and furnishings inside, put together by Dollmann, Seitz and another theatre designer, Christian Jank, allude everywhere to the House of Bourbon, from the statue of Louis XIV in the Hall to the sumptuous King's Bedchamber. The park, landscaped by Karl von Effner, is adorned with an ornamental lake; a tall fountain; a primitive *Hundinghütte* (where Ludwig would quaff mead, pretending to be a thane); one of the King's beloved Moorish kiosks (with the spectacular peacock throne designed by Seitz) and, of course, the Grotto. This famous piece of theatrical architecture, with lighting effects by electricity, was built by the landscape gardener August Dirigl; the boat and other props were again designed by Seitz.

Next, Ludwig II, a 'high camp' figure if ever there was one, carried to excess his mania for the past by recreating Versailles on an island in the Chiemsee which

75 The Winter Garden on the roof of the Munich Residenz. Ludwig II's first executed building was an iron and glass construction rather in the style of Paxton's Crystal Palace. Begun in 1867, it was extended in 1869 and again from 1870 to 1871; the designer was Karl von Effner and the backdrop scene of the Himalayas was painted by the stage artist Christian Jank. The whole effect is indeed that of a theatre set.

76 (*above*) Linderhof: the 'Dream King's' favourite residence, seen from the marble rotunda above the south garden. This '*Petit Trianon*' was constructed around one of his father's wooden hunting-lodges in Upper Bavaria, between 1872 and 1878. The architect was Georg Dollmann and the grounds were laid out by Karl von Effner. In the middle of the pool below is a gilded group of Flora and her nymphs by Wagmüller; the jet of water rises to nearly 100 feet in height.

77 (*right*) The Moorish Kiosk at Linderhof, an unlikely object to come across in the mountains of Bavaria, was bought by Ludwig II in 1876 from the owner of Schloss Zbirow in Bohemia. It is thought that the Kiosk, of cast iron and walled with zinc plaques, probably came from Paris where the Moorish style was then in vogue. Ludwig also had similar kiosks installed at Schloss Berg and in the Winter Garden at the Residenz, Munich.

he had bought in 1873. Building work for this favourite project (known as 'Meicost-Ettal', an anagram of '*L'état c'est moi*') finally got under way five years later. First Dollmann, then Hofmann faithfully carried out the wildly extravagant scheme to restate the message of Versailles. Although the west façade, the staircase, the State Bedchamber and, of course, the Hall of Mirrors aim at reproducing the palace of the revered Sun King, not all of Herrenchiemsee is slavish imitation. The Marble Court to the east, though in the Louis XIV style, was a new creation and such creations as the Porcelain Room and King's Guard Room, with its muted marble plaques and parquet flooring, were more agreeably original. The perils of working for Ludwig are illustrated in the terrible story of the designer Otto Stoeger, who was literally driven insane by his attempt to find exactly the right blue for the globe of the lamp in the king's bedroom at Herrenchiemsee. Ludwig stayed here just once, for ten days.

Neuschwanstein cost 6,180,047 marks, Linderhof 8,460,937 and Herrenchiemsee 16,579,674. It is hardly surprising that the Bavarian Government regarded the King's building activities with alarm, particularly as his plans for building still more and larger castles threatened to bankrupt the country. The irony is that since Ludwig II's death his palaces have paid for themselves many times over as showplaces; they are indeed the *raison d'être* of the booming Bavarian tourist industry.

78 Herrenchiemsee: the Marble Court on the east façade designed by Georg Dollmann in a Louis XIV style. The foundation stone was laid in 1878.

As Ludwig II's brother Otto was already hopelessly insane and behind bars, it was easy for the ministers to persuade themselves that he was going the same way. His eccentricities, such as his nocturnal torch-lit sleigh-rides through the mountain valleys and the command theatre performances for him alone in the Munich Residenz, had lifted eyebrows for years. In 1886, the Government appointed a leading 'alienist', Dr Bernhard von Gudden, to report on the mental condition of the king; and Gudden duly pronounced him insane without examination. A commission consisting of Gudden and other doctors, together with various officials, was then sent to Neuschwanstein to take the king away into captivity. After being ignominiously repulsed by the local peasantry, who rose with scythes and axes in defence of their king, the commissioners made a second attempt to seize Ludwig and were this time successful; he was removed to the lakeside castle of Berg. Meanwhile, his uncle, Prince Luitpold, was appointed Regent. On the day after his arrival at Berg, Ludwig went for a walk with Gudden in the castle grounds. A few hours later, the king's body and that

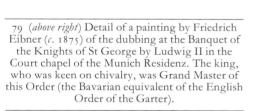

79 (*above right*) Detail of a painting by Friedrich Eibner (*c.* 1875) of the dubbing at the Banquet of the Knights of St George by Ludwig II in the Court chapel of the Munich Residenz. The king, who was keen on chivalry, was Grand Master of this Order (the Bavarian equivalent of the English Order of the Garter).

80 (*right*) The Grotto in the grounds of Linderhof must rank as the most theatrical of all Ludwig II's stage-struck architecture. Built 1876–7 by the landscape gardener August Dirigl, it was adorned with a cockle-boat and other props by the theatre designer Franz Seitz. The extraordinary lighting (blue for Capri, red for Tannhäuser), the artificial waves and the other *coups de théâtre* owed much to electricity. 'I don't want to know how it works,' said the Dream King, 'I just want to see the effects.'

of Gudden were found in the lake. What happened, and whether Ludwig's intention was to commit suicide, or merely to escape from his captors, will never be known.

Prince Luitpold's grandson, Crown Prince Rupprecht, resumed life at Nymphenburg and the other Bavarian royal palaces when the Wittelsbachs returned to Munich after the 1918 Communist uprising. Even if the throne was officially abolished, Rupprecht was still, to all intents and purposes, King of Bavaria. Although a rugged military man, he inherited his family's cultural brilliance, being an expert on Indian and Chinese art.

In 1933, there was a move to restore the Bavarian monarchy, as a means of counteracting the influence of Hitler; and when this was found to be unconstitutional, there was the idea of appointing Rupprecht as *Staatskommissar*. Nothing came of this, either, and Rupprecht continued to be no more than an unofficial monarch. During the Second World War he was forced to leave Bavaria and went into hiding in Italy. By the time of his death, at the age of 86, Rupprecht had become a legend. During his last years, he lived once again in his ancestral palaces; he would appear at a window of the Munich Residenz and be cheered by the crowd. On the occasion of his 85th birthday, crowds from the capital went out to greet him at Nymphenburg, singing the Bavarian national anthem and shouting 'Long live our lawful King!' Rupprecht's son, Duke Albrecht, is the senior living descendant of James I of England and VI of Scotland, or in other words the Stuart claimant to the British throne.

The head of another German royal house, Prince Ernst August of Hanover, is the senior lineal descendant of the Hanoverians who replaced the Stuarts on the British throne; indeed, had the Salic Law applied in Britain the Prince would now be king in place of Queen Elizabeth II.

In 1692 Duke Ernest Augustus of Hanover was raised to the Electoral dignity and the ceremony took place in the banqueting-hall of the family palace on the Leine river. Built about 1640, the Leine Schloss had been greatly improved by Ernest Augustus after his coronation as Duke of Hanover in 1680. His wife Sophia (a sister of Prince Rupert the Cavalier and a granddaughter of James I of England) was a noted patron of the arts, commissioning Gobelin tapestries depicting scenes from the life of her mother Elizabeth, the 'Winter Queen' of Bohemia. During the renovation and redecoration of Leine Schloss other tapestries and pictures were brought from Holland, the interior of the chapel was gilded and a new opera-house was built. The philosopher Leibnitz became court librarian and Hanover basked in a flowering of culture.

Duke Ernest Augustus's predecessor had planned a summer residence at Herrenhausen, inspired inevitably by Versailles. Ernest Augustus and, especially, Sophia, followed up the idea enthusiastically. The palace is no more, having been bombed in the Second World War, though happily the gallery built by Johann Wachter with frescoes of the *Aeneid* by Tommaso Giusti escaped destruction. Herrenhausen's best feature has also survived: the Baroque garden described as 'my very life' by the Electress Sophia. The gardens were laid out by Carbonet from 1696 to 1710 under the influence of Le Nôtre and it is possible that the great man himself may have had a hand in the plans. The orangery, with its glass panels, was a remarkable innovation when glasshouses were still a rarity. As well as providing the ducal table with fruit out of season, it also became Electress Sophia's favourite retreat. The gardens at Herrenhausen, which are worthy of comparison with those at Versailles and Schönbrunn, have long been celebrated and it is on record that the visitors have included Peter the Great, the Duke of Marlborough and his friend Prince Eugene (of Belvedere fame).

In 1714 the Elector Ernest Augustus's son George Ludwig became King George I of Great Britain. A century later the title of 'King of Hanover' was assumed on behalf of George III of Great Britain and the two crowns remained united until the accession of Queen Victoria in 1837. Then, because the crown of Hanover was subject to the Salic Law (and therefore could not be inherited by a woman), it passed to Queen Victoria's eldest surviving uncle, Ernest Augustus, Duke of Cumberland.

In the interim Hanover had been ruled by viceroys and it was a source of gratification to the new king's subjects when Hanover once again came to be the seat of a royal court. The Leine Schloss was renovated in a neo-Classical style to the designs of Georg Laves, the surveyor-general. Ernest Augustus's court was brilliant and well-organized, and also extremely hospitable, though he had very simple tastes and was inclined to regard the more elaborate court ceremonial as humbug. To people who, when speaking to him, began with the traditional form, 'Allow me to throw myself at Your Majesty's feet!' he would retort, 'Rubbish! If you did, you would split your trousers!'

When revolutionary fever swept Europe in 1848, a mob advanced on the Altes Palais to demand concessions from the King. Ernest Augustus, who was now not far off 80, lay ill in bed in his room on the ground floor of the palace, with only a frosted-glass window between him and the angry rabble on the pavement outside. But he remained perfectly calm and refused to accede to the demands of the mob, which soon dispersed.

In 1853 Bismarck visited Ernest Augustus's son, King George V of Hanover. The 'Iron Chancellor' was struck by the helplessness of the blind king. The room where the king did business was dimly lit, for he naturally did not notice when the candles burnt down to their sockets, and no servant came in to replace them. 'The table at which we were sitting was so littered with every imaginable sort of public and private papers', Bismarck recalled, 'that as the King moved about several of them fell to the ground and I had to pick them up. No less remarkable was it that the blind King should transact business for hours at a time with a strange diplomatist like myself, without any minister to take cognizance.'

The consequence of this observation by Bismarck was the annexation of the kingdom of Hanover by Prussia in 1866. However, there was a twist to the story when the blind king's grandson, Prince Ernst August, Duke of Cumberland, married the Kaiser's daughter in 1913. The wedding was one of the last great royal occasions of old Europe. The celebrations ended with the *Fackeltanz* or torch dance, a dance only performed at German royal weddings in which nobody below the rank of Royal Highness was allowed to take part. Preceded by pages bearing lighted silver candelabra, the dancers progressed in threes round

82 Herrenhausen, Hanover. 'That garden is my very life,' wrote the Electress Sophia about the Baroque grounds laid out by Carbonet from 1696 to 1710. The palace itself, remodelled in the early 1820s by General Georg Laves, was bombed in the Second World War, though the gallery built by Johann Peter Wachter in 1696 has survived.

the Weisser Saal – probably the last time that this dance was ever performed in the Berlin Schloss.

After the collapse of the German monarchies at the end of the First World War, the last Wettin king of Saxony was once on a train journey in his former kingdom and was greeted at a station by a crowd of his ex-subjects, who asked him to show himself at the window of his carriage. Frederick Augustus looked down at the smiling crowd with a grin and called out: 'Well, I must say, you *are* a fine set of Republicans!'

This down-to-earth monarch was noted for his plain speech. Once, at a royal gathering, Frederick Augustus asked the Kaiser whether he intended to wear uniform or plain clothes in the evening during a visit he was about to make to the Archduke Franz Ferdinand. The Kaiser thought and then said that he imagined he would wear uniform. 'Quite right!' exclaimed the cheerful king. 'You look hideous in plain clothes!'

83 The Zwinger, Dresden: a series of pavilions (begun in 1711) linked by single-storeyed arcaded halls, the masterpiece of the Baroque architect, Matthäus Daniel Pöppelmann. Like many another German monarch, Augustus 'the Strong' of Saxony was fascinated by Versailles.

The homeliness of King Frederick Augustus of Saxony was in marked contrast to the splendours of his royal palace at Dresden, famous for its Zwinger (or outer courtyard), with its rich Baroque curves and undulations. The palace was built at the turn of the eighteenth century by Augustus 'the Strong', that larger-than-life figure described by Carlyle as 'The Ever-Cheerful Man of Sin'. Augustus kept a harem and left 354 bastards – including, incidentally, a direct ancestor of George Sand, the novelist – though he found it difficult to keep track of his love-children and at least one of his daughters subsequently became his mistress. During his time as the elected King of Poland he used to impress his dinner guests by picking up two of his State trumpeters, one in each hand, and holding them out at arm's length for five minutes, while they played a fanfare.

For all his lechery, gluttony and brawn Augustus was a splendid patron of the arts who beautified Dresden and presided over the Meissen porcelain factory. In 1703, together with his architect Dietze, Augustus planned a stupendous project for rebuilding the royal palace so that its garden would stretch down to the banks of the River Elbe. Unfortunately Dietze died the following year, and only a fragment of the great scheme was ever executed. This was the Zwinger built by the master of Saxon Baroque, Matthäus Pöppelmann, from 1709 onwards. Ten years later the Zwinger was still in a half-finished state when it was used for the festivities to celebrate the nuptials of Augustus's only legitimate son to the Emperor's dwarfish daughter.

When the happy pair arrived in Dresden, Augustus the Strong mistook a very pretty young lady-in-waiting for the bride, and embraced her with paternal fervour. Then, discovering his mistake, he turned to his son and said coldly, '*Monsieur, j'aurais cru que vous auriez eu meilleur goût*' ('Sir, I would have thought you had better taste'). Needless to say, the old roué consoled the lovely lady-in-waiting for not being his daughter-in-law by making her his mistress.

Bellotto's pictures provide vivid evidence of the Zwinger's use as a pleasure parade for court ceremonial and pageantry: we see elegant courtiers and their carriages. The Zwinger consists of a great court surrounded by a gallery and seven pavilions. The decorative sculpture is principally by Pöppelmann's collaborator Balthasar Permoser. Sir Sacheverell Sitwell has described the Zwinger as 'one of the strangest products of the Late Renaissance, quite unlike anything else in history till the Paris Exhibition of 1900'. In his view the whole affair is a kind of prelude to Art Nouveau. This extraordinary building was yet another German royal palace to be badly damaged in the Second World War, although, again, the restoration has been laudably conscientious so that the Zwinger is now an important museum.

Pöppelmann also built a courtyard castle for Augustus the Strong at Pillnitz on the Elbe in the early 1720s and then transformed an old hunting-lodge at Moritzburg into another Baroque castle (now a museum). The fourth Saxon palace, Hubertusberg, also began life as a hunting-lodge in the 1720s to the designs of Johann Naumann.

In 1743 Augustus the Strong's only legitimate son and namesake had Hubertusberg completely rebuilt by Knöffel with a tower, a chapel, commodious wings and high, wide, arched windows. The younger Augustus

had a passion for the arts and for collecting pictures which was even greater than his father's. He was not pleased when Frederick the Great sent a detachment to clear Hubertusberg of its contents and sell them in aid of Prussian field hospitals. This unfriendly behaviour was provoked by the looting of Charlottenburg by Saxon soldiers and by Augustus's characteristic sloth in not replying to Frederick's subsequent letter of remonstration.

When Bismarck noted in the course of his scheming for German unity that he had an audience with King William I of Württemberg 'in the chimney corner at Stuttgart', he may have unintentionally conveyed the impression of homeliness. Nothing could be further from the truth, for the grandeur of the Stuttgart Schloss and the formality of the Württemberg court were proverbial. The Altes Schloss, originally a thirteenth-century moated castle, had been enlarged in Renaissance style for the Dukes of Württemberg in the sixteenth century; and the vast Baroque Neues Schloss had been begun in 1744 to the designs of Leopoldo Retti. Duke Karl Eugen, the builder of the new palace, wanted it to be in the '*neuen Gout der Architektur*' ('new style of architecture'). After Retti's death in 1751 the building was carried on by Pierre-Louis-Philippe de la Guêpière.

84 (*above left*) The Zwinger, Dresden: detail of the wall pavilion by Matthäus Daniel Pöppelmann.

85 (above) Stuttgart: the *Neues Schloss* built from 1744 onwards in what Duke Karl Eugen of Württemberg described as the new style of architecture. The architects were Leopoldo Retti and, after 1751, Pierre-Louis-Philippe de la Guêpière.

Since the Second World War this official residence of the former kings of Württemberg has been restored and its palatial state rooms are now used for municipal receptions.

Every country seems to have its Versailles and Württemberg's is Ludwigsburg, the biggest Baroque palace in Germany. This magnificent edifice was built between 1704 and 1733 for Duke Eberhard Ludwig of Württemberg, to the designs first of Johan Nette and after his death in 1714 to those of the Italian architect Donato Frisoni. Set in a park ten miles outside Stuttgart, Ludwigsburg has formal gardens and large expanses of lawn. The exterior is of golden stone with pavilions linked by galleries. The east pavilion contains a games-room ingeniously hidden in the dome where the duke and his cronies

86 Schloss Solitude, the House of Württemberg's
country palace near Stuttgart.

87 Ludwigsburg, near Stuttgart: the biggest Baroque palace in Germany, built between 1704 and 1733 for Duke Eberhard Ludwig of Württemberg.

could play cards in seclusion. The most curious of the hundreds of rooms at Ludwigsburg is the raffish duke's bedroom, a *cabinet d'amour* (with ubiquitous mirrors placed at all sorts of angles and gold figures leaving little to the imagination) which he had copied from seventeenth-century Dutch originals.

The architect of the Neues Schloss in Stuttgart, Guêpière also built two charming country palaces for the House of Württemberg in the 1760s, Schloss Solitude and Mon Repos. Solitude has a Baroque theme of a central oval room with lower wings and adjoining end pavilions. Mon Repos has a similar oval room but with a vestibule in front. As in the Amalienburg pavilion at Nymphenburg, the projecting oval on the garden side of Mon Repos is counterbalanced by a concave centre on the entrance side.

The most prominent feature at Schloss Solitude was probably King Frederick I of Württemberg's stomach. His desk, duly hollowed out to accommodate the majestic girth of the man who was made a king by Napoleon in 1806, is still on view here. After describing the beauties of one of the royal family's summer retreats at Friedrichshafen on Lake Constance, Princess Mary Adelaide (mother of Princess May of Teck, the future Queen Mary of Great Britain) wrote: 'But oh the stiffness of the inmates!'

By the time of King William II at the end of the nineteenth century the court at Stuttgart was positively *gemütlich*, thanks to his second wife Charlotte whom May of Teck found 'too jolly and off-hand for a Queen, and so ugly besides'.

Shortly before the Kingdom of Württemberg was swept away with other German monarchies by the First World War, the young Prince of Wales (later Edward VIII) paid a visit, which he subsequently recalled:

> For a *Königspaar* Onkel Willie and Tante Charlotte were sympathetic and easygoing. Their ample figures betrayed the justice they did to their four full meals a day. . . . After an enormous lunch, almost every fine afternoon the King and Queen took a leisurely drive through the suburbs of Stuttgart in an open victoria, and sometimes I was summoned to drive with them. Under the influence of the warm sun and the gentle motion of the carriage, Onkel Willie would quickly fall asleep, only to be constantly aroused by a swift jab of the Queen's elbow to acknowledge the salute of one of his soldiers, the precise salutation of a stolid Württemberger, or to straighten the Homburg hat that kept sliding rakishly to one side of his head. This process had been going on for so many years that, when Onkel Willie got that dig in his well-padded ribs, he was able to straighten his hat in his sleep.

Great Britain

88 (*previous page*) St James's Palace: the Tudor gateway built by Henry VIII in about 1535. After the burning of Whitehall in 1698 this building became the metropolitan palace of the sovereign. A new block of state rooms was built to Wren's designs on the south side overlooking St James's Park; these were later embellished by William Kent and others, including William Morris & Co, who carried out a redecoration in 1866. (*See pages 114, 116*)

89 The Queen's House, Greenwich: the entrance front facing the river, with the Observatory in the background. Begun for James I's queen, Anne of Denmark, the Queen's House was the first important architectural commission of Inigo

When he saw the Baroque grandeur of Blenheim Palace, the magnificent gift of a grateful sovereign to the triumphant Marlborough, George III remarked that he had 'nothing to equal this'. He had a point. When he came to the throne in 1760, the British royal residences were fairly few and in general considerably less spectacular.

The old Palace of Westminster, with its surviving medieval Great Hall, had ceased to be a royal residence after the disastrous fire of 1512. The Tower of London, begun by William the Conqueror in 1078 and lived in by various medieval sovereigns, no longer had a proper royal court by early Stuart times. Although William the Conqueror's other stronghold, on the Thames at Windsor, had been notably developed by Henry II (who built the royal lodgings in the Upper Ward), Edward IV (who built St George's Chapel), Elizabeth I (who built a long gallery) and, above all, by Charles II (who reconstructed the Sovereign Apartments in magnificent style, with carvings by Grinling Gibbons and ceilings painted by Verrio), the castle had been neglected by the first two Georges. Eltham Palace in Kent, a favourite residence of several medieval kings, had fallen out of favour from the time of Henry VIII and had been allowed to decay.

Greenwich, the palace for which Henry VIII had forsaken Eltham, remained a royal residence only until the end of the seventeenth century. Henry VIII, the founder of the British Navy, spent large sums in making the riverside Greenwich a 'pleasant, perfect and princely palace'. Later the first of the Stuart kings in England, James I (VI of Scotland), gave it to his queen, Anne of Denmark, as a peace-offering after he had scolded her too severely for accidentally shooting his favourite hound. The queen then commissioned Inigo Jones to build her a miniature palace bridging the public road from London to Woolwich, which separated the main palace from its park.

Before the Queen's House, as it came to be known, was finished, Anne of Denmark was dead, but it was completed and furnished for her daughter-in-law, Queen Henrietta Maria, wife of Charles I. With its perfect Classical proportions, Ionic loggia, painted ceilings by Jakob Jordaens and Orazio Gentileschi, its gilded decoration and bust of Charles I by Bernini, it must have been the most elegant and sophisticated house of its time in England – a testimony to Charles I's exquisite taste and love of the arts. The widowed Henrietta Maria returned to the Queen's House after the Restoration in 1660, and Jones's nephew, John Webb, was employed to enlarge it. Charles II also commissioned Webb to rebuild the main palace, but this was unfinished at the time of his death in 1685. Ten years later Greenwich was given over to the Royal Hospital for Seamen. Mary II, however, insisted that the view to the river from the Queen's House should not be obscured, and so the Royal Hospital was finally built in the form of twin palaces, flanking the much smaller Queen's House in the centre. Henry, Earl of Romney, who became Ranger of Greenwich Park in 1667, moved the road to its present line between the Queen's House and the Royal Hospital, but the arches through which it formerly passed under the house can still be seen. After being used for various purposes, the Queen's House has recently been beautifully restored and redecorated.

Jones, the great English Palladian. It was completed between 1629 and 1635 for Charles I's queen, Henrietta Maria, with a superb interior. It is now the National Maritime Museum, flanked by the Royal Hospital for Seamen.

Richmond Palace, where Elizabeth I died, was partly dismantled during the 'Commonwealth' of Oliver Cromwell and was eventually parcelled into tenements. Henry VIII's half-timbered Nonesuch Palace in Surrey also disappeared in the late seventeenth century and the whole conglomeration of buildings that formed the royal palace of Whitehall went up in smoke in 1698, owing (it was said) to the carelessness of a Dutch laundrymaid – all, that is, save for the Banqueting-House, designed by Inigo Jones with a ceiling painted by Rubens. Through one of its upper windows Charles I stepped out on to the scaffold in 1649.

Charles I had the taste but not the resources to bring the projected new palace in the capital (of which the Banqueting-House was the only part to be built) into being. At the beginning of the seventeenth century Whitehall had grown into a warren of lodgings, galleries, courtyards and gardens stretching for nearly half a mile along the bank of the river. It was not just the principal London residence of the king, but the seat of government of a state that was growing increasingly

90 Whitehall: the Banqueting House. James I's first effort at a banqueting house as a setting for the court masques was burnt down in 1619; in its place Inigo Jones built this perfect Classical double cube (110 feet by 55 feet). The ceiling panels were painted by Rubens. Commissioned by Charles I when the great artist was in England in 1629, the panels were painted in Antwerp and completed in 1634. They show the apotheosis of James I and his 'Divine Right'. The Banqueting House is a solitary reminder of the magnificent palace the Stuarts planned to build at Whitehall.

complex, with dependencies overseas. Londoners regarded Whitehall as 'mean and inelegant', and in 1619 James I initiated a scheme for rebuilding it, with Inigo Jones as architect. Jones and his nephew John Webb produced designs for a palace which, in its final form, was one of the grandest architectural concepts of the Renaissance, enclosing seven courtyards including a circular 'Persian Court' and covering an area twice the size of the Escorial, but which, unfortunately for posterity, was far beyond the exchequer of both James and Charles I. With the outbreak of the Civil War, the scheme was finally dropped.

Apart from his works at Greenwich and Windsor, Charles II's most ambitious project was at Winchester, which, after his experience of the London mob during the Exclusion crisis, he contemplated making his capital. Here, Wren began to build him a palace that would have outdone Hampton Court as the 'English Versailles'. It was to have had colonnades and cupolas, high enough for the king to see his warships riding at Spithead; it would have been approached by a street 200 feet broad leading from Winchester Cathedral, lined on each side with noblemen's houses. The palace was just about to be roofed when Charles's death put a stop to the whole scheme; in the nineteenth century, the surviving buildings were made into barracks.

George III, however, had only himself to blame for the lamentable absence of Hampton Court from the centre stage of state in the late eighteenth century. It was he who abandoned what is architecturally the finest palace in the possession of the British Crown. After Henry VIII had picked it up from Cardinal Wolsey, the butcher's boy from Ipswich who overreached himself, Hampton Court remained a much-loved royal residence for the next five reigns. Mary I and Charles II both spent their honeymoons here; Shakespeare and his company acted in the Great Hall before James I, and also perhaps before Elizabeth I.

Hampton Court was less frequently occupied from the time of Charles II onwards; but William III so liked its situation that he commissioned Wren to rebuild it. The project, however, was incomplete at the time of King William's death in 1702 (caused by a riding accident after his horse had stumbled on a molehill here). The result is that today there is the pleasing contrast between the gateway, courtyard, Great Hall and gallery dating from Tudor times and the partially-built Wren palace that lies beyond them, with its grand front facing along the canal and its ranks of state rooms.

George II (r. 1727–60) was the last sovereign to live at Hampton Court. He carried on the bad Hanoverian family tradition of quarrelling with his eldest son and on one notorious occasion 'Poor Fred', the Prince of Wales, removed his wretched wife from the palace when she was in an advanced stage of labour so as to prevent his mother from being present at the birth. George III fell foul of his grandfather, George II, in one of the state apartments at Hampton Court and received a sound box on the ears. According to the Duke of Sussex, George III's son, this painful experience so coloured his feelings for the palace that he decided never to darken its doors again.

George III also deserted Kensington Palace. At the end of the seventeenth century William III had bought the house of the former Lord Chancellor, Heneage Finch, Earl of Nottingham, near the village of Kensington, in order to

provide himself with a residence where he could breathe the country air, but which was closer to London than Hampton Court. It henceforth came into prominence as the 'Court Suburb'. The Kensington Palace of today, elegant and comfortable in its warm red brick, is largely the work of Wren, who, with Nicholas Hawksmoor as his clerk of works, rebuilt Nottingham House after it had been purchased by the king. William III's three successors on the throne all preferred Kensington to their other palaces. Queen Anne built the Orangery, according to Vanbrugh's or Hawksmoor's design; while during the reign of George I, William Kent added a new set of state apartments, as well as the King's Staircase: its walls are painted with courtiers and ladies, pages and Yeomen of the Guard, looking down from *trompe-l'oeil* balconies. Kensington eventually came into prominence again as the house where Queen Victoria spent her childhood. In later years it was also the childhood home of Queen Mary, who, after her husband had ascended the throne as George V, considered the possibility of making Kensington the London residence of the king and queen,

91 Hampton Court Palace: Wren's south front, which was built between 1689 and 1694. Views have varied as to the contrast between the romantic and the classical in the architecture of the palace. James Pope-Hennessy observed that from 'an interesting monument of the English Renaissance, Hampton Court was transformed into a Dutch copy of Versailles'.

92 Hampton Court Palace: the Queen's Drawing-Room, which was decorated by Antonio Verrio for Queen Anne in 1705. Above the chimney-piece her unsatisfactory husband, Prince George of Denmark, Lord High Admiral of England, points to the fleet. On the ceiling, the queen receives the homage of the four quarters of the globe. The paintings were covered up in 1741 and only rediscovered in 1899. The state bed, which was made for the ample Queen Anne, is upholstered in cut velvet.

in preference to Buckingham Palace. Now the Prince and Princess of Wales make their London home at what the previous Prince of Wales used to call 'the Aunt Heap'.

George III preferred a series of rather unpretentious villas in Richmond and Kew to Hampton Court and Kensington, though at different times he did commission both Sir William Chambers and James Wyatt to produce designs for palaces nearby. George III also embarked, in a fairly modest manner, upon the Gothicizing of Windsor Castle with the help of James Wyatt, his surveyor-general. He did not get very far before succumbing to the horrible disease now believed to be porphyria. At the time, of course, he was merely considered to be off his head.

Incidents like the one observed by a page called Philip Withers in the Great Park at Windsor tended to confirm people's worst suspicions. While out driving with the queen, George III suddenly pulled the horses up, descended from the carriage and approached an oak-tree, proceeding to shake it by one of the lower

branches and carry on an earnest conversation under the impression that it was the King of Prussia. Withers was glad to report, however, that 'His Majesty, though under a momentary dereliction of reason, evinced the most cordial attachment to freedom and the Protestant faith'. Sadly, the periods of instability grew more frequent until by 1811 the king was permanently insane.

In 1762 George III had bought Buckingham House, built at the beginning of the eighteenth century for John Sheffield, Duke of Buckingham, according to the designs of William Talman and the Dutch architect, Captain William Winde. With its spacious grounds, more like a country-house park than a town garden, Buckingham House was the finest private house in London, but not on the scale of a royal palace. There was a celebrated 'house-warming' after the king had made a few improvements to Buckingham House, with the grounds being illuminated by 4,000 coloured lamps and a vast coloured picture of George III showing this unlikely figure dispensing peace to all the world.

The comparatively modest scale of Buckingham House appealed to George III who occupied it as his London residence while using St James's for ceremonial. After the burning of Whitehall in 1698 St James's became what it still officially is: the metropolitan palace of the sovereign. It is to the 'Court of St James's' that ambassadors are accredited.

93 (*above*) Hampton Court Palace: the Great Gatehouse of the Tudor front. Built by Cardinal Wolsey from 1514, the palace was acquired by Henry VIII fifteen years later. The gatehouse was in fact rebuilt when it was in danger of collapse between 1770 and 1772, in the Tudor style, re-using the roundels of Roman emperors by Giovanni da Maiano. Nothing conjures up the world of the Tudors so colourfully as Hampton Court, with its red brick and elaborate chimneys.

94 (*right*) Kensington Palace: the King's Staircase. This was the last of this palace's interiors to be completed by William Kent in the 1720s. The *trompe-l'oeil* paintings represent an open colonnade behind which a motley crew observe the visitors mounting the stairs. Some of these figures can be identified, such as George I's two Turkish *valets de chambre*, and Peter the Wild Boy, who had been discovered as a child of about thirteen years, walking on his hands and feet in the woods of Hanover, 'with the agility of a squirrel'. On the ceiling, Kent painted a self-portrait, and 'a beautiful actress' with whom 'he lived on terms of intimacy'.

St James's Palace is on the site of a medieval hospital (for 'fourteen leprous maiden sisters, living chastely and honestly in divine service') which enjoyed the right to hold a May fair in the neighbouring fields – the origin of 'Mayfair'. After the fire at the Palace of Westminster Henry VIII acquired this Convent of St James the Less from its custodians, Eton College. Of the palace he built here, little now remains save the familiar gateway facing up St James's Street, which bears the ciphers of Henry and Anne Boleyn, and dates the structure to about 1535 when that queen was still in favour. Wren enlarged the state apartments towards the park which were embellished by later architects, notably William Kent. At one *levée* a bowing Scots colonel's kilt rode up his back causing George III to cry out: 'Keep the ladies in front. Keep the ladies in front!'

Even with Kent's embellishments St James's and, more to the point, Kensington were absurdly modest compared with Schönbrunn, Caserta, the Oriente in Madrid and the other royal palaces which, during the first half of the eighteenth century, were springing up in or near most European capitals. Indeed, there was many a margrave or prince-bishop in Germany who could boast of a new Rococo *Residenz* that far exceeded Kensington Palace in grandeur. The first three Georges were less splendidly housed than some of their own subjects, although, paradoxically, there was a greater degree of formality at the Court of St James's than at most other eighteenth-century courts. At various times during the century there were plans for giving London the sort of royal palace which the growing wealth and power of Britain seemed to demand: thus Kent provided George II with designs for a rather dull palace in Hyde Park. But during the reign of Farmer George and his homely consort Queen Charlotte the tendency was in the opposite direction.

Cometh the hour, cometh the man: George IV, a royal builder in the grand manner, made up for his father's love of simplicity. He had taste, like Charles I and Charles II; but unlike them, he was able to bring his schemes into being. In 1783, at the age of 21, long before he became king or even prince regent, he started to transform Carlton House, his official residence, into the most spectacular palace London had yet known – the masterpiece of Henry Holland, after whose death it was completed by Wyatt, John Nash and Thomas Hopper. The exterior – the Corinthian entrance front, guarded by its Ionic screen, facing up what is now Lower Regent Street, and the garden front overlooking St James's Park – had something of Holland's characteristic restraint. But within, all was of the utmost splendour: columns of porphyry or yellow Siena marble, with bronze or silver capitals; walls hung with crimson damask; a circular drawing-room with the ceiling painted like the sky, from which crystal chandeliers cascaded down and were endlessly reflected in pier glasses; a Gothic dining-room. By the time he became king, George IV had grown bored with this palace of enchantment; and a few years later, he ordered it to be pulled down. Fortunately, however, his other extravagance, the Brighton Pavilion, a royal fantasy that compares only with Henry VIII's Italianate Nonesuch, is still there for us to enjoy. The colourful and exotic furnishings of this royal pleasure dome have been restored – though when Queen Victoria, who associated it with the

95 Windsor Castle. The Lower Ward is dominated by the Gothic perpendicular St George's Chapel (built from 1472). The entrance to the Lower Ward was rebuilt by Henry VIII (the gatehouse is still named after him). Windsor was transformed into the place we see today (in this panoramic view) by Sir Jeffry Wyatville. The Long Walk (completed by George IV) stretches away to the right of the picture. The state apartments are situated principally on the north side of the Upper Ward (above the Home Park); the royal family live on the east side overlooking the formal gardens (at the top of the picture).

more raffish side of her uncle's career, gave it up, its future must have been very
much in doubt. The Prince Regent commissioned Nash to build him this vision
of the gorgeous East in 1815, the year of Waterloo. The style is at once Chinese
and Hindu, with a saucy dash of Tartar. Inside it is a riot of red and gold, of
dragons and bamboos, pagodas and banana foliage.

For all his profligacy and spoilt behaviour George IV had style, wit and
imagination. Above all, he gave the British monarchy a suitably magnificent
background – something which it had hitherto lacked, owing to the shortage of
money of the Stuarts, the early Georges' lack of interest and his parents'
frugality. Buckingham Palace and Windsor Castle, as they are today, are largely
his creation.

At Windsor George IV transformed the place by restoring a 'medieval' air to
the castle. This tremendously ambitious enterprise was undertaken by the
nephew of James Wyatt, Jeffry Wyatville. His name was originally Wyatt but he

96 Brighton Pavilion. 'It is as though St Paul's had gone down to the sea and pupped,' said Sydney Smith about George IV's multi-domed vision of the gorgeous East. First, in 1787, Henry Holland and then, in 1815, John Nash were commissioned to work on this exotic 'Marine Pavilion' (originally a farmhouse) for the prince of pleasure. The interior was dismantled in the 1840s, but in 1849 the pavilion was bought by Brighton corporation who have since restored this unique phenomenon with great attention to detail and with much élan.

had asked George IV if he could adopt this somewhat affected nomenclature to avoid confusion with the other architects in the family. 'Veal or mutton, call yourself what you like,' the king is said to have replied. Sir Jeffry (as he became) gave the Upper and Middle Wards a Gothic appearance by the romantic additions of curious windows, corbels and crenellations.

Purists find much of Wyatville's work at Windsor ugly and absurd but no one can deny that, at least from a distance, the overall picture is enchanting, indeed everything a castle should be. Over his sixteen years of work from 1824 onwards, Wyatville achieved a remarkable symmetry and unity.

Sir Jeffry also redesigned much of the interior, thereby sacrificing all but three of Charles II's interiors. He doubled the length of St George's Hall by absorbing a former chapel; this handsome room rests on the fourteenth-century vaulting of Edward III's old palace, and it is interesting to note that the masonry of its walls remains unchanged from the days when the first Knights of the Garter feasted there. Wyatville also built the Grand Corridor (550 feet long) joining the east front to the south front. George IV was the first king to use the east front for his private apartments – a tradition actually begun by Queen Charlotte and continuing to this day – leaving the north front as the state apartments.

The best known of the state apartments is the Waterloo Chamber which the king planned towards the end of his reign to commemorate Wellington's mighty victory. The chamber was erected on the site of an open court in the centre of the north front which lies alongside parts of the castle inhabited by the sovereign from the earliest times, and much of its masonry dates from the first stone buildings put up by Henry II in the twelfth century. The Waterloo Chamber is sumptuously decorated and displays a grand series of portraits of the monarchs, soldiers and statesmen who contributed to the downfall of Napoleon; some thirty of them are by Sir Thomas Lawrence.

George IV's other achievement at Windsor was the completion of the Long Walk. Hitherto a cluster of buildings had prevented the avenue from stretching right up to the castle walls but the king razed these, including a house designed by his father, to the ground. Perhaps to make up for this, he commissioned an imposing statue of George III, in the inappropriate garb of a Roman emperor, astride a gigantic copper horse, which was placed as an eye-catcher at the far end of the Long Walk.

When George IV ascended the throne in 1820 he was determined to give the capital the imposing royal palace which it had hitherto lacked. He therefore commissioned Nash to turn 'Buck House' into a palace large enough for royal entertaining. Nash built the new palace round a three-sided courtyard, the open side facing the Mall and approached through a triumphal arch. The main front overlooked the garden, and incorporated the shell of the original house. Unfortunately, the Duke of Buckingham's painted staircase and his other interiors were not preserved; but Nash's state apartments are certainly well suited to their purpose. The architect managed to recreate something of the sumptuousness of Carlton House – particularly the Blue Drawing-Room, with its Siena columns, and the Music Room, with its bold reliefs of *putti* in the spandrels of the domed ceiling.

97 Windsor Castle: the Waterloo Chamber. Sumptuously decorated by Wyatville, this triumphal room displays a series of portraits of the monarchs, soldiers and statesmen who contributed to Napoleon's defeat at Waterloo in 1815. Some 30 of the portraits are by Sir Thomas Lawrence – including that of George IV himself who was prone to reminisce, in his cups, about his own (totally fictitious) part in the battle. Every year a Waterloo Banquet is held here.

98 Osborne: the Durbar Hall, which was added in 1890 to celebrate Queen Victoria's function as Empress of India. The Indian decoration was designed by Bhai Ram Singh; Rudyard Kipling's father, John Lockwood Kipling, was consulted about the initial plans. The Durbar Hall came in particularly handy as a place to put the assortment of presents given to the Empress by eastern potentates.

99 (*above*) Buckingham Palace: the garden front of Bath stone. This was the principal façade of John Nash's rebuilding for George IV, which was unfinished by the time of the king's death in 1830. The work was carried on by Edward Blore (who removed Nash's dome) and by Nash's nephew, Sir James Pennethorne, who had added the south wing (to the right of the picture) containing the State Supper Room and the vast Ballroom by 1855.

100 (*left*) Windsor Castle: the Queen's Presence Chamber. This is one of only three surviving interiors from the time Charles II reconstructed the Sovereign Apartments between 1675 and 1678 to the designs of Hugh May. The ceilings were painted by Antonio Verrio, the Italian artist, who was brought from Paris by the Duke of Montagu; the carvings are by Grinling Gibbons and the gilding by René Cousin.

101 (*right*) Buckingham Palace: the White Drawing-Room. Finished in 1831, this 48-foot-long room overlooks the gardens and the lake. The frieze by William Pitts shows the 'sports of boys'. The cut-glass chandelier, with an ormolu framework, has 24 candle-shaped lights; the candelabra include two pairs of the Louis XIV period. The pilasters, originally of Siena scagliola, were 'Frenchified' by C. H. Bessant in the time of Edward VII, whose Danish queen, Alexandra, is portrayed above the fine chimney-piece.

Both George IV and Nash were dead before Buckingham Palace – as it finally came to be known, having at times been called St George's and also, sarcastically, 'Pimlico' Palace – was completed. Queen Victoria and Prince Albert found it inconvenient and lacking in accommodation. At one time there was even the idea of adapting it for some cultural use and building a new palace elsewhere. Instead, Edward Blore provided rooms for the Queen's growing family by enclosing the courtyard with a rather dull range facing the Mall – Nash's triumphal arch being banished to Tyburn, where it became familiar to later generations of Londoners as the Marble Arch. Then Sir James Pennethorne added the south wing containing the vast Ballroom and Supper Room, which was not completed until 1855.

Six years later occurred the death of the Prince Consort and so the palace was deserted for much of Queen Victoria's long widowhood. In 1873 it was lent to the Shah of Persia for his state visit and there were some bizarre antics. Apparently the Shah took his meals on the floor, was reluctant to avail himself of the palace's lavatories and organized a boxing-match in the garden. It has even been suggested that he had one of his staff executed with a bowstring and buried in the grounds. Such a happening would have been in keeping with the story of how, when looking round an English prison on a later state visit, he was shown the gallows and asked whether he could see it in use; on being told there was nobody who was to be hanged, he said, 'Take one of my suite!'

Buckingham Palace cannot be said to have come really into its own until within living memory, when it was the setting for the brilliant Drawing Rooms and Court Balls held by Edward VII and Queen Alexandra. After George V and Queen Mary had dropped the idea of returning to Kensington, the Mall front

102 (*above left*) A 'still' of a film photographed at Balmoral in 1896 by, in Queen Victoria's words, 'the new cinematograph process, which makes moving pictures by winding off a reel of films'. Here the queen herself takes a 'turn in the pony chair'. At her feet sits her granddaughter, Princess Patricia of Connaught (later Lady Patricia Ramsay, the water-colourist); Tsar Nicholas of Russia stands by the front of the chair. To the right of Queen Victoria are the Duchess of Fife; the Tsarina; the Duchess of Connaught and Princess Margaret of Connaught.

103 (*above centre*) Holyroodhouse: the Gallery. The 111 portraits of Scottish monarchs were painted by the Dutch artist Jacob de Witt between 1684 and 1686. He was paid a salary of £120 a year for his trouble in painting such imaginary likenesses as Fergus Mor MacErc who established the Scottish kingdom of Dalriada at the end of the fifth century. In 1745 the gallery was the scene of Bonnie Prince Charlie's State Ball before his victory at the battle of Prestonpans; it is still used for banquets by the Lord High Commissioner to the General Assembly of the Church of Scotland.

104 (*above right*) 'Dear old Sandringham' (as George V called it) in the snow. Although Prince Albert had the offer of the great Palladian palace of Houghton in Norfolk when he was looking for a country house for his eldest son, they settled on Sandringham in the same county. In 1870, after tinkering with the existing structure on the site, Albert Edward, Prince of Wales (later Edward VII), rebuilt the house in 'Jacobean' style to the designs of A. J. Humbert. R. W. Edis made additions in 1883 and again in 1891 after a fire.

was given a more imposing façade of Portland stone designed by Sir Aston Webb; it is this façade of 1913, rather than Nash's work, which for most people signifies Buckingham Palace.

As well as completing Buckingham Palace, Queen Victoria contributed to the saga of the royal residences by purchasing an estate in the Isle of Wight and another in Aberdeenshire, and building a large country house on each – the Italianate Osborne and the Scottish Baronial Balmoral. The idea of the monarch leading a simple country life as a change from pomp and circumstance was, of course, nothing new; but whereas George III's rural retreats had been near London, and adjacent to an old royal park, Osborne and Balmoral were in parts of the country which had no traditional connexions with the sovereign. Moreover, they belonged to the queen as a private individual, whereas previous royal residences had all been Crown property. As another new departure, Prince Albert was himself largely responsible for the design of both houses, assisted respectively by the great London builder, Thomas Cubitt, and by William Smith (son of 'Tudor Johnnie') of Aberdeen. The 'tartanitis' and thistles as decorative motifs were too much for some visitors. Lord Rosebery remarked that he had considered the drawing-room at Osborne to be the ugliest in the world until he saw the one at Balmoral; while Lord Clarendon pointed out that 'the thistles are in such abundance that they would rejoice the heart of a donkey if they happened to look like his favourite repast which they don't'.

Osborne later became unique among the royal residences in having a room specially dedicated to Queen Victoria's new function as Empress of India: the Durbar Hall. The state and private apartments at Osborne remain furnished as they were in Queen Victoria's time, though the rest of the house was given up by

105 Holyroodhouse, Edinburgh: the west front, with Arthur's Seat to the right. In the foreground is the James IV Tower begun in 1501 and completed under James V of Scotland between 1529 and 1532. The palace was rebuilt after Charles II's Restoration under the supervision of Sir William Bruce. From 1671 to 1680 the south-west tower was built to complement the James IV Tower and a handsome façade placed between the two.

106 Balmoral Castle: the Scotch Baronial structure of Prince Albert and his architect William Smith by Loch-na-Gar. Finished in 1855, the castle was built of Invergelder granite and boasted turrets, castellated gables, a *porte-cochère* and a 100-foot tower. The landscaping was by James Giles. 'My heart', wrote Queen Victoria in her journal, 'becomes more fixed in this dear paradise and so much more so now that *all* has become my dearest *Albert's* own creation . . . his great taste and the impress of his dear hand have been stamped everywhere.'

Edward VII to be a convalescent home for officers. He already had a country house of his own in England: Sandringham, rebuilt for him in the 'Jacobean' style when he was Prince of Wales, on the Norfolk estate which he had acquired largely for the shooting.

Queen Victoria's decision to spend part of every year at Balmoral was greatly welcomed by the Scottish people, who had seen little of their sovereigns since James VI ascended the English throne as James I. One alone among the ancient royal palaces of Scotland has continued to be the abode of her kings and queens down to the present time, though it was deserted for long periods in the past. This, of course, is Holyrood in Edinburgh, crouching below the cliffs of Arthur's Seat at the opposite end of the Royal Mile from the Castle. It was originally built between 1501 and 1503, for the reception of Margaret Tudor, the bride of James IV, adjoining an abbey of Canons Regular founded by David I in 1128. The abbey church became the Chapel Royal, which has been a ruin since the roof collapsed in the eighteenth century. Much of the palace was burnt while it was occupied by Cromwell's troops; the parts that survived include Mary Queen of Scots' apartments, the scene of the particularly grisly murder of her secretary David Rizzio. A new quadrangle was built by Charles II, under the supervision of Robert Mylne and to the design of Sir William Bruce of Kinross. Owing to shortage of money, its style was austere, the plain walls being relieved in places by typically Scottish turrets. Inside, however, were rich furnishings and tapestries; the gallery was adorned with a hundred fanciful portraits of Scottish kings, painted at £2 a head by an enterprising artist named Jacob de Witt.

During the eighteenth century, the most notable royal visitor to Holyrood was Prince Charles Edward Stuart, the Young Pretender. The old palace saw nothing of the Georges until George IV held court here in 1822; inspired by Sir Walter Scott, the ample George donned a kilt, wearing flesh-coloured tights to preserve his modesty. The king revelled in it all, being cheered to the echo by crowds estimated at a million as he drove in state to and from Holyrood, where some 2000 people were presented to him at a *levée*. Scott, who acted as master of ceremonies, reported that 'the visit of the King to Edinburgh ... was like the awaking of Abou Hassan to a dream of Sovereignty'. Possibly overcome with emotion, the king stumbled on the staircase at Holyrood but was saved from a nasty fall by the shoulders of a stout baronet.

Queen Victoria started the custom, continued by her successors, of occupying Holyrood for a brief period every year. For all its somewhat forbidding appearance, Holyrood is one of the most atmospheric of royal palaces, little changed from the time of Charles II and with a combination of intimacy and grandeur that is particularly Scottish. Its special character is enhanced on state occasions by the presence of the Royal Company of Archers in their picturesque green uniform, many of them descended from forebears who frequented the palace in the days before the Stuart kings deserted it for Whitehall, Windsor and Hampton Court.

Greece and the Balkans

After the Greeks had disentangled themselves from the Turks to become an independent kingdom in 1830, there remained a problem: who was going to be king. The crown was twice hawked around the courts of Europe, with a republican spell intervening, and eventually was offered to Prince Leopold of Saxe-Coburg, the former son-in-law of George IV of Great Britain. He, however, preferred to become King of the Belgians. Next the Greek crown was offered to Prince Otto, second son of the King of Bavaria, who accepted it in 1832.

The young Bavarian prince was chosen as a compliment to his father, King Ludwig I, an ardent Philhellene who had not only supported the cause of Greek independence, but made Greece fashionable. He was busy adorning Munich, his capital, with splendid public buildings in the neo-Grecian style. Unfortunately the new Greek king completely failed to understand the Greek temperament. Not only did he see fit to protect himself with Bavarian troops, which may have been necessary in the climate of the times; but he had Bavarian ministers, who endeavoured to govern the unruly sons of Hellas with a German bureaucracy.

King Otto also made himself unpopular by maintaining a much grander court than his poor and underdeveloped country could afford. Having moved his seat of government to Athens, he built himself a huge and costly palace, in an austere and rather Germanic neo-Grecian style. It might have been one of his father's Classical buildings in Munich, transported to Greece. Indeed, it was by his father's principal architect, Friedrich von Gartner, and King Ludwig I duly laid the first stone in 1836. Finished in 1842, it was given a Doric portico in Pentelic marble on the west front and an interior decorated in the Pompeian manner. For a long time the palace was the only impressive building in Athens, apart from the ruins of antiquity; it rose stark and massive above what was little more than a tumble-down village.

Here the king – wearing a white kilt in the fashion of his subjects, or 'an elaborately embroidered Greek dress of blue and silver' – and his queen, the beautiful Amalie of Oldenburg, lived in somewhat comfortless grandeur, surrounded by an army of aides-de-camp in scarlet and gold. They held court balls in the manner of the Munich *Residenz*: but as most Greek women disliked dancing, there were seldom more than three couples on the ballroom floor and the men – many of them in their everyday clothes, with neck-clothes and boots – outnumbered the women by four to one. The queen, in addition to being beautiful, was as well-intentioned as her husband; but she, too, was disliked. Not only did she fail to produce an heir; she incurred the resentment of the inhabitants of Athens by creating the lovely palace garden, which used up too much water in summer when it was scarce. And the Greeks, whose outlook was in some ways still Oriental, were shocked by a queen who went riding, or worse, went for long and strenuous walks in the country, her Greek maids of honour panting behind her.

After a revolution in 1842, Otto was obliged to dispense with his Bavarian troops and to grant a Constitution – commemorated to this day in the name of the square in front of the royal palace (which is now the Greek Parliament). Twenty years later, following another revolution, the king and queen went back

to Bavaria, as it turned out for good. Thus began the first in-and-out phase of Greek monarchy.

The Greeks then chose a new king by popular vote. Poor Otto received only one vote and the clear winner was Queen Victoria's second son, Prince Alfred (later Duke of Edinburgh and of Saxe-Coburg and Gotha), though he was soon found to be ineligible as belonging to the ruling house of one of Greece's 'Protecting Powers'. Instead of a British prince, the Greeks settled for the brother of the future Queen Alexandra of Great Britain, Prince William of Glücksburg. The first intimation to this younger son of the heir to the Danish throne that he had been elected King of Greece was from the greasy newspaper wrapping of a sardine sandwich in the lunch-packet which he took with him to the Naval Academy.

So Prince William of Glücksburg was transformed into King George I of the Hellenes, having adopted the most Hellenic of his Christian names. The young king did not repeat the mistakes of his predecessor but he was under no illusions as to the difficulties of staying on the throne of this turbulent country, telling his ministers that (like Leopold of the Belgians) he 'kept a portmanteau ready packed'. He strengthened his position both in his own country and in the entire Slavonic world by choosing a Russian bride, the Grand Duchess Olga, niece of Tsar Alexander II. To set the seal on her popularity, the queen gave the country five princes and two princesses, all of them born and brought up in Greece.

The king and queen and their large family lived a happy but very simple life; for then, as later, the Greek royal house was not at all rich. They spent much of their time at Tatoi, a heavily-wooded estate in the country which the king bought in 1871. Here he built a house rather like a large Swiss chalet and gathered together antiquities from the estate to form a museum. Tatoi was their home rather than Otto's great German-Grecian palace in Athens, which they found 'excessively uncomfortable' and bitterly cold in winter.

Nevertheless, the royal family found the palace's vast ballroom was a good place for roller-skating and indoor cycling. The king, followed by his whole family in order of seniority, would weave in and out of the pillars in fine style. This was not, however, the only use to which the ballroom was put. For there were often court balls and other entertainments; but these were less formal and much more democratic than in Otto's day. Knowing the democratic ideas of his subjects, King George I kept the etiquette and ceremonial of his court down to a minimum. This informality was for ever afterwards a characteristic of the Greek monarchy.

When he became king, George I brought Greece the Ionian islands which Britain had given him as an accession present. The Palace of St Michael and St George in Corfu was duly handed over by the British High Commissioner to serve as an additional royal residence for the new king. A large Classical building, the palace was designed in 1819 by Colonel George Whitmore of the Royal Engineers to serve as the treasury for the newly created Most Distinguished Order of St Michael and St George (an order of knighthood awarded for service overseas, particularly in diplomacy) and as a residence for the Lord High Commissioner. The colonel (later General Sir George Whitmore) had an awkward time of it, as he recalled: 'I was forced to model almost every particle of the building, and I think there were no less than eight or nine different languages spoken by the workmen.' The wretched sapper was not even told that he had to incorporate the chamber of the Ionian legislative assembly into the palace until after his design had been approved.

All things considered, Colonel Whitmore did a splendid job. The exterior, of Malta stone, has a Doric portico of 32 columns; above the cornice are seven sculptured medallions representing the Ionian islands. The interior is decorated in the Adam manner, the most beautiful room being the circular hall which divides the Throne Room from the State Dining-Room. This well-proportioned composition has a domed roof set with plaques of Wedgwood blue, and Classical statues in niches around the walls.

The Palace of St Michael and St George was used occasionally by George I but fell into disrepair after his assassination at Salonika in 1913. It was eventually well restored in 1956 by the Corfiot architect Jean Collas and now houses a collection of Sino-Japanese art. The other royal residence on Corfu was Mon Repos which had served as a summer retreat for the British Commissioners and continued to be used for the same purpose by the Greek dynasty. An elegant neo-Classical villa, it was built at the same time as the Palace of St Michael and St George. The chief claim to fame of Mon Repos is as the birthplace of Prince Philip of Greece and Denmark, a grandson of King George I, who married the Queen of Great Britain. Prince Philip was born here on 10 June 1921; the actual delivery took place on the dining-room table.

King George I's successor, Constantine I, found himself in a difficult position in the First World War when he tried to remain neutral. Because his queen was the Kaiser's sister, the king was accused of being pro-German, but this was not in fact the case. The queen aptly described herself as being 'in a horrible no-man's land of distraction'. The Allies, with the connivance of the Greek Prime Minister, set about undermining the king's authority by means of an army of secret agents.

The terrible forest fire at Tatoi in 1916 is believed to have been these agents' doing. Eighteen of the royal household lost their lives, and the king and queen and two of their children only escaped death by a narrow margin. George I's museum of local antiquities was also consumed in the conflagration. Then Allied warships in the Piraeus bombarded the royal palace in Athens, so that the queen and her children had to take shelter in the cellars. Constantine I was ordered to abdicate by France; as the eldest son had received his early military training in Germany, his second son succeeded to the throne.

The new king, Alexander, was virtually a prisoner in his palace. In the autumn of 1920, however, he was staying at Tatoi when he met his death at the age of 27: while he was walking in the gardens, his dog was attacked by a pet monkey belonging to the vineyard-keeper. He tried to separate the two animals, and was bitten by the monkey. Blood poisoning set in, and he died after a month of ever-increasing pain. While he lay dying, his mother begged from her exile in Switzerland for permission to go to him; but the Government would not allow this. So easy is it for facts to be distorted that it came to be believed that the

109 (*below*) Belgrade, Yugoslavia: the 'Frenchified' royal palace famous for its defenestrations.

monkey had belonged to King Alexander himself; and it was held up as a sign of his irresponsibility that he should have been playing with pet monkeys when Greece was in such a critical state.

The box-and-cox history of the Greek monarchy continued with the return of Constantine I following a plebiscite; then came another abdication; a revolution that ousted the new king, George II, and confiscated all royal property; and a return in 1935 after another plebiscite. After the fall of Crete in the Second World War, George II went into exile once more and his return was delayed through Communist pressure until another plebiscite in 1946. When he saw on the tape-machine at his home-from-home in London, Claridge's Hotel, that of the 303 inhabitants of a village near Athens, 301 had voted for his return, George II's normally impassive features dissolved into tears. In view of the frequent reversals of fortune in the Greek royal house it would be a rash man who predicted that the present head of the dynasty, King Constantine II, will not be seen again in the royal residences of Greece.

One of the palaces of Greece connected with the Hellenic royal family, Rhodes, was rebuilt by the Italians during the Second World War with an eye to it being used as a summer residence for that ill-matched pair Victor Emmanuel III and Mussolini. The diminutive Italian sovereign was married to the Junoesque daughter of King Nikola of Montenegro, a little mountain state in the Balkans.

Nikola, who assumed the title of king in 1910, was one of the most picturesque European sovereigns of his day, frequently clad in the colourful Montenegrin national dress. Descended from a line of prince-bishops (or *Vladikas*) who ruled as a theocracy, Nikola succeeded his non-ecclesiastical uncle, the Prince of Montenegro, in 1860. His capital, Cetinje, was no more than a small village, but as Nikola's key position in the Balkans became increasingly crucial in the 'Great Game', almost every other house was a legation. The king's palace, a modest two-storeyed villa, was built from 1863 to 1871 and then remodelled in 1910.

We can glimpse Cetinje as it was shortly after the end of its royal era through the eyes of the British colonial administrator Sir Harry Luke. On his visit he was struck by the air of melancholy that pervaded the former royal capital, 'now the *chef-lieu* of an outlying and rather hungry province'. With the departure of the court and the diplomatic corps, the inhabitants had lost their main source of livelihood. The king's palace and the legations were closed and empty. The interior of the palace was even more depressing than the shuttered exterior; for nothing in it had been touched since the day that the royal family left. Portraits of the Petrovic dynasty and of foreign sovereigns hung askew on the walls of the reception rooms, where the paper was beginning to peel; the king's diamond-hilted sword was 'lying carelessly on the billiard-table'; there were clothes still hanging in the cupboards and gramophone records scattered about the princesses' boudoir.

A few years earlier, in 1918, the Conference of Ambassadors in Paris had united the kingdom of Montenegro with that of the Serbs, Croats and Slovenes. This new state became known as Yugoslavia. Its first sovereign was Alexander,

110 (*bottom*) Bucharest, Roumania: the neo-Classical royal palace built between 1930 and 1937 by the erratic Carol II of Roumania.

of the Serbian Karadjordjević line, who did his best to unite his heterogeneous kingdom; but the task was well nigh insuperable – it was said that the only real Yugoslavian was the king himself. Shabbily treated, like other continental monarchies, by the Allies in the Second World War, the Yugoslav monarchy was not restored after Tito's partisans had established the Communist base for a republic.

The royal palace in Belgrade, a Frenchified structure with a couple of domes which has been compared to the casino at Monte Carlo, was the scene of the defenestration in 1903 whereby the Karadjordjevićs ousted their long-time rivals the Obrenovićs from the Serbian throne. On a hot and sultry night in June the 'Black Prophecy', by a peasant who had forecast the extinction of the Obrenović dynasty, came true. Troops surrounded the palace and a party of officers (who had hatched a conspiracy to overthrow Alexander Obrenović and put Peter Karadjordjević on the throne) forced their way into the building in search of King Alexander and Queen Draga. Finding them hidden in a secret chamber off their bedroom, they shot them down, and slashed them with their swords. Then, with a cry of 'Long live Peter Karadjordjević, King of Serbia!' and a wild whoop, the officers threw their two victims out of the window into the garden below, for the soldiers to see. The bodies of Alexander and Draga lay exposed on the grass while the officers celebrated at tables in the palace courtyard, drinking the health of Peter Karadjordjević in wine from Alexander Obrenović's cellar. Eventually the Russian minister arrived on the scene and suggested that it would be more seemly for the bodies to be taken indoors.

After the Second World War the Communists also put paid to the monarchy of Roumania, 'liberating' no less than nine El Grecos from the Hohenzollern dynasty which had reigned here since 1866. Prince Karl of Hohenzollern-Sigmaringen was metamorphosed into King Carol I of Roumania and he in turn transformed a backward and impoverished Turkish province into a wealthy European state. His wife was the romantic poet 'Carmen Sylva' (otherwise Queen Elizabeth), nicely summed up by her successor as 'both splendid and absurd'. She used to stand, at all hours of the day and night, on the terrace of her house overlooking Constanza harbour calling out blessings to the departing ships through a megaphone. Carmen Sylva liked to surround herself with a circle of writers, artists and musicians – including one old charlatan who imagined that he could sing equally well in tenor, baritone or bass – to whom she would listen in hand-clasped rapture.

The modern story of the Roumanian monarchy is inevitably dominated by the erratic behaviour of Carol II, who ran away with 'Zizi' Lambrino in 1918, then after an annulment married Princess Helen of Greece, only to elope a few years later with the flame-haired temptress Elena Lupescu. For all his faults, however, Carol II was an enthusiastic patron of the arts and in the 1930s he rebuilt Bucharest according to his own taste. The royal palace was revamped in a sort of neo-Classical style by N. Neuciulesco with marbled interiors, an Imperial staircase, an Adamesque dining-room and a theatre seating 112. The main attraction in the palace (now used by the Roumanian government) remains the imposing Throne Room, with its El Greco *Adoration of the Shepherds*.

The Balkan state of Bulgaria was created by the Congress of Berlin in 1878; but, as was the way in these troublesome parts, its first sovereign, Prince Alexander of Battenberg, did not last long. As the doting Queen Victoria recorded, life was made impossible for 'poor brave Sandro' by 'these Russian fiends'; he abdicated in 1886.

When Prince Alexander took up residence in the royal palace in 1878 he found this former seat of the Beylerbey of Sofia in a lamentable condition. Young Sandro's slumbers were said to be disturbed by plaster falling from the ceiling on to the princely bed. The palace was accordingly renovated and remodelled in the 'Bulgarian Renaissance' style (with Baroque touches here and there) to the designs of the architects Grünenger, Lars and Meyerbeer.

The royal palace at Sofia was considerably enlarged by 'Ferdy the Fox', the Coburg prince who became Prince of Bulgaria in 1887 and proclaimed himself King Ferdinand of the Bulgarians in 1908. As a sybarite, an aesthete and a fop – there is a description of him in his younger days wearing a light grey suit, 'an ultra chique Panama hat' and 'smart yellow boots', constantly waving his well-manicured hands to display the costly rings that glittered on his fingers – Ferdy

111 The Bulgarian royal palace at Sofia. Formerly the seat of the Beylerbey of Sofia, it was remodelled in the 'Bulgarian Renaissance' style to the designs of Grünenger, Lars and Meyerbeer after the arrival of Prince Alexander in 1878. 'Ferdy the Fox' later enlarged the palace, which is now the National Gallery of Art and Ethnographic Museum.

112 (*above*) Tirana, Albania. King Zog, wearing the white cockade, surveys the scene from the balcony of his somewhat modest royal palace. The Albanian monarch always believed in having plenty of protection, as this picture demonstrates.

113 (*right*) Tirana: the Red Salon in the royal palace.

seemed a most unlikely candidate for the throne of so primitive and politically violent a country as Bulgaria. Queen Victoria predicted that he would not last in Sofia a year; in fact, he reigned for over 30 years and lived to be 87.

Sofia was laid out afresh, with main drainage, and adorned with heavily ornate and imposing public buildings. The royal palace was considerably enlarged, with emphasis being placed on the monumental Throne Room on the first floor. Today the palace is given over to the National Gallery of Art and the Ethnographic Museum. The Communists abolished the monarchy in 1946, sending the young King Simeon and his mother into exile. King Simeon's father, King Boris, had once said that he had no fear of losing his throne through revolution because he could always get a job in the United States as an engineer or a college professor. Railway engines were his passion; Edward VIII of Great Britain recalled how, when he was taking his leave of King Boris and Prince Kyril, who had travelled with him in his train as far as the Yugoslav frontier, the farewells were somewhat perfunctory owing to an argument between the Bulgarian monarch and his brother as to who should drive the engine of the train that was waiting to take them back to Sofia.

The kingdom of Albania was not created until just before the First World War when yet another German princeling, William of Wied, unwisely accepted the new crown. The courts of Europe christened him *Le Prince de Vide*; sure enough, he and his wife Sophie departed within a matter of months, losing all their possessions in the process – including Sophie's harp. The next sovereign was the legendary Zog, formerly Ahmed Zogu, the country's energetic president, who was proclaimed King of the Albanians in 1928. King Zog moved the capital inland from Durazzo to Tirana, a Moslem village consisting of a bazaar and four gaily-coloured mosques. Soon it became what Cetinje had been in the days when Montenegro was an independent kingdom: a village where almost every other house was a legation. Zog set about transforming it into a modern capital city, aligning new roads, laying out public gardens, planting avenues of trees.

The new royal family lived in a well-to-do merchant's house in Tirana while Zog planned a suitable palace as a background for his majesty. But by the time this was ready for occupation, Zog, his family and a formidable entourage of bodyguards had gone into an exile which was to stretch from the early part of the Second World War, when he was based at the Ritz Hotel in London, to the king's death in Paris in 1961. Meanwhile, in 1946, the Communists had abolished the monarchy in Albania which had been assumed by King Victor Emmanuel III of Italy following the Italian invasion in 1939.

The Netherlands, Belgium & Luxembourg

114 (*previous page*) Colmar Berg, Luxembourg, which was transformed from a hunting-lodge by German architects for Grand Duke Adolphe in the 1890s. The *château*, noted for its gardens, remains the family home of the Grand Duke. (*See page 150*)

115 (*below*) Het Loo, Apeldoorn, was built from 1685 to 1692 by Jacob Roman for William III. Formerly the residence of the late Queen Wilhelmina, Het Loo is no longer used by the Dutch royal family.

The kingdom of the Netherlands (known as Holland from the old countship of that name in its centre) came into being in 1815; it developed out of the seven United Provinces that had revolted against Spain in the sixteenth century. In 1830 the southern portion of the Dutch kingdom broke away to become the modern kingdom of Belgium and in 1890 the Grand Duchy of Luxembourg, which had been in union with the kingdom of the Netherlands since the Congress of Vienna in 1815, passed to a senior branch of the House of Nassau.

The last Count of Holland was William 'the Silent', Prince of Orange and Stadholder of Holland and Zeeland, who was encouraged to take the title in 1580 after he had led the revolt in the Netherlands against the Habsburg kings of Spain. Count Philip III of Holland, otherwise King Philip II of Spain, had precipitated this unrest by his oppressive methods of keeping the Dutch in order, and particularly by religious persecution, after the Reformation. Something of the uncompromising Spanish attitude towards these Calvinist colonials can be deduced from the fact that in 1568 the Inquisition condemned all inhabitants of the Netherlands to death as heretics. After William the Silent's assassination in 1584 the Countship of Holland was never revived, but his descendants continued to govern the Netherlands as Stadholders and this office was eventually declared hereditary in the Orange family in the late seventeenth century.

The former castle of the Counts of Holland in The Hague is today the home of the Dutch parliament. Most of the buildings, a rather haphazard group, though on medieval foundations have been either restored or completely reconstructed. The first castle was begun in 1250 by Count William II who had previously been elected King of the Romans. Half-a-dozen years later, on the point of heading south to be crowned Emperor in Rome, he was drowned during an expedition against the West Frisians. Rather inappropriately, perhaps, in view of his watery demise, the Count is commemorated by a nineteenth-century fountain-statue outside the central building of the Binnenhof. This central building is the late-thirteenth-century Knights' Hall (much restored) which now houses the first and second chambers of parliament. The first chamber, built by Pieter Post in 1660, has a fine ceiling and an allegorical chimneypiece (on the fitting theme of War and Peace) by Jan Lievens and Adriaen Hanneman. The second chamber was built from 1777 to 1790 as a ballroom for Prince William V of Orange, father of the first King of the Netherlands.

It was at The Hague that Elizabeth I's erratic favourite Robert Dudley, Earl of Leicester, resided during his fairly futile governorship of the United Provinces in the 1580s. The main line of Dudley's companion-in-arms, William the Silent, expired in 1702 with the death of the most famous Orange prince of all, William III. His mother was the Princess Royal, eldest daughter of King Charles I of England, and he married his first cousin Mary with whom he jointly ascended the English throne in 1689. Although not popular in England, William III was nevertheless a European statesman of the first magnitude and was respected as such by Louis XIV.

Four years before acceding to the English throne, William (he was William III of both his Dutch principality and his English kingdom) had begun building the

116 (*bottom*) Mauritshuis, The Hague, which has been the Royal Picture Gallery since 1821. Built 1633–44, it is one of the first Dutch buildings to show the Italian Classical influence, and was designed by Jacob van Campen.

palace of Het Loo, outside Apeldoorn, to the designs of Jacob Roman. Daniel Marot had a hand in the interiors and gardens. Earlier in his reign as Stadholder, William had commissioned Maurits Post to build him a hunting lodge at Soestdijk near Baarn.

William III died in 1702 having expressed a wish to pass on the Stadholdership to his cousin, Jan Willem Friso, Prince of Nassau-Dietz, who succeeded in becoming Stadholder of only a couple of provinces. The Stadholdership was, however, again made hereditary in all seven provinces for his son William IV, son-in-law of George II of Great Britain. Then William V was driven out of the Netherlands by the French, sailing to England in a fishing boat in 1795.

The French occupation of the Netherlands lasted for nearly twenty years, during which time the House of Orange came to symbolize the Dutch people's resistance against the French yoke ('*Oranje boven!*' – 'Up Orange!' – was the cry heard when there were anti-French riots). In 1806 Louis Bonaparte was placed on the Dutch throne by his brother Napoleon, but displeased the Emperor by apparently being prepared to put the welfare of his new subjects before everything else and was obliged to abdicate in 1810. The Netherlands were then absorbed into the French Empire.

The architectural legacy of Louis Bonaparte's brief reign was the conversion by the French king of the old town hall of Amsterdam into a royal palace. Built in 1648 to the designs of the leading contemporary Dutch architect, Jacob van Campen (with a little help from Daniel Stalpaert), the town hall expressed municipal might in a thumping structure of six storeys and 23 bays, with a wide pedimented centre. The chief merit of this rather overpowering monument of Dutch classicism lies in the sculptural decoration by Artus Quellin, who portrayed the merchant city of Amsterdam surrounded by Neptune and his attendants in the pediment, as well as decorating the huge (four-storeyed) marble hall inside with another allegory of Amsterdam among Strength, Plenty and Wisdom. The statuary remains the most outstanding feature of the royal apartments, though the Throne Room boasts an important painting by Ferdinand Bol. The apartments are still used when the Queen of the Netherlands is in Amsterdam and the Council Hall makes one of the most outstanding banqueting rooms in Europe.

After Napoleon's defeat at Leipzig, the provisional Dutch government invited Prince William VI, the 'Old Frog' (so called because he was the father of the 'Young Frog', the future King William II, whose sobriquet derived from his broad forehead, bulging blue eyes and wide mouth) to return from exile in England as sovereign prince. In 1815 he was proclaimed King of the Netherlands, as William I, as well as Grand Duke of Luxembourg. His new kingdom also included the former Austrian Netherlands (now Belgium).

To provide a suitable background for the Orange-Nassau monarchy in addition to the royal palaces of The Hague, Het Loo and Amsterdam, King William I enlarged the old hunting lodge of Soestdijk from 1816 onwards to the designs of Jan de Greef. As a summer residence the King used Het Huis ten Bosch outside The Hague, originally built for the daughter-in-law of William

117 Het Huis ten Bosch, The Hague. The central block was designed by Pieter Post in 1645; Daniel Marot added wings in 1734. The palace has recently been restored as the home of Queen Beatrix.

the Silent in the middle of the seventeenth century. For much of the nineteenth century this exquisite palace was the scene of the intellectual *salon* presided over by Queen Sophie, wife of King William III (son of the Young Frog). One of William III's brothers, Prince Hendrik, has a place in social history as the first member of European royalty to go on a pleasure trip to India. He went there in 1837, when he was 17, and his presence was a source of great pleasure to the Governor-General's chef, who had known him as a child when he was cook in the royal palace at The Hague.

On William III's death in 1890, his ten-year-old daughter, Princess Wilhelmina, succeeded him as Queen of the Netherlands, whereas the Grand Duchy of Luxembourg passed to the Duke of Nassau, in accordance with the Salic Law and the Nassau family pact. Soon after her accession, Queen Wilhelmina paid a visit to Queen Victoria, who is reputed to have said to her young guest, when everyone else had withdrawn: 'As we're two Queens together, we can say what we like!'

118 Soestdijk, the home of Queen Juliana, the Queen Mother, between Soest and Baarn. The central block was designed by Maurits Post as a hunting-lodge for William III in 1674. King William I enlarged the building to the designs of Jan de Greef in 1816.

Queen Wilhelmina came of age in 1898 and reigned for the next fifty years, a wise and much-loved sovereign who became the symbol of her people's resistance during the two World Wars in much the same way as her forebears had done in the days of the French occupation. She preferred to spend her summers at Het Loo rather than Het Huis ten Bosch and retired to the former after her abdication in 1948. Het Loo is no longer used by the royal family.

Wilhelmina's successor, Queen Juliana, decided to live at Soestdijk (where she still resides as Queen Mother) and to use Het Huis ten Bosch for official meetings and occasions of State. However, Queen Beatrix made it clear, when she took up her duties upon her mother's stepping down, that she would prefer to live close to the political and diplomatic life of The Hague. Thus Het Huis ten Bosch has recently become the principal residence of the Dutch royal family.

Het Huis ten Bosch was begun in 1645 by Prince Frederick Henry to the designs of Pieter Post, a Palladian enthusiast, and completed by the Prince's widow, Amalia, as a glorified memorial to her husband who died in 1647. She decorated the central hall, the *Oranjezaal*, with allegorical paintings by Jordaens, Honthorst, Van Thulden, Gonsales Coques, van Everdingen, Willeboorts, Jan Lievens, de Grebber, de Bray and others; Rembrandt's estimate for a contribution, alas, was regarded as too high. The themes reflected Prince Frederick Henry's life, and particularly his military triumphs in the Thirty Years' War, painted in the manner of Rubens. The brilliant *trompe l'oeil* effect of movement and illusion was co-ordinated by the architect van Campen (of Amsterdam town-hall fame), who had an unenviable time coping with the artists. Jordaens seems to have been the most captious, though he failed in his attempts to have the figure of Death removed. The *Oranjezaal* is the only room at Het Huis ten Bosch to survive as it was in Amalia's time; as a memorial to her husband it stands as a monument unique in European architecture.

Het Huis ten Bosch was tranformed from what was essentially a summer house into a palace in the 1730s by the son-in-law of George II of Great Britain, Prince William IV of Orange and Nassau-Dietz. The veteran French Huguenot architect Daniel Marot enlarged the place in the Baroque manner by adding wings at an angle to either side of the forecourt. The wings contained elaborate suites of apartments such as the surviving White Dining Room, in the west wing, with its *trompe-l'oeil grisailles* of the chase by Jacob de Witt.

Other rooms in the palace, such as the neo-classical Green Room which contains gilt furniture and a charming portrait of the future King William I and his young siblings, tend to be of later date. Their father, Prince William V, was given two sumptuous apartments at Het Huis ten Bosch by a loyal subject who must have done very well for himself running the Dutch East India Company at Canton. Princess Wilhelmina wrote to her daughter in July 1791:

> We have received superb presents from China from a M. Emminkson, who has brought back suites of furniture for two or three rooms of satin embroidered in colour on a white background, a service of porcelain for tea, for coffee and for chocolate, comprising 1,454 pieces, with our arms and nothing else except a border in white and gold in the taste of the porcelain from Sèvres, as well as a whole number of beautiful things in lacquer. I really find this present too magnificent, and am almost ashamed to accept it.

The Stadholder and his wife managed to force themselves to do so, however. This magnificently generous gesture comprised the Japanese and Chinese Rooms at Het Huis ten Bosch.

Since August 1981, Het Huis ten Bosch has been both a setting for official receptions and a home for the queen's family. The original central block has been reserved for state rooms, while the two wings have been rearranged and redecorated: the left for the family, the right for guests and officials. State dinners are held in the White Dining Room. It is a terrible thought that under German occupation in the Second World War plans were laid to demolish Het Huis ten Bosch, but one can now rejoice that this palace is, so to speak, beatified under the present queen.

Queen Beatrix's neighbouring sovereign, King Baudouin of the Belgians, divides his time between the Château de Laeken in the suburbs of Brussels, which is home, and the royal palace in the city centre, which is the office. Set in a sizeable park, Laeken was originally built in the 1780s for Princess Marie Christine of Austria, Governor-General of the Austrian Netherlands with her husband Prince Albert of Saxony. It was later refurbished for Napoleon, who gave Laeken a place in the history books by signing the order there for the advance of his armies into Russia in 1802; and it had to be rebuilt in 1890 after a disastrous fire. Today it is best known for its splendid hot-houses which King Baudouin opens to the public every spring, though the rest of the palace remains very much a private residence for himself and his Spanish wife Queen Fabiola.

119 Het Huis ten Bosch, The Hague: the *Oranjezaal*. Decorated by followers of Rubens with allegorical paintings, this central hall which rises to the roof of the building was completed by Princess Amalia as a memorial to her husband.

The heir to the Belgian throne is the King's brother Prince Albert, Prince of Liège, who lives opposite the entrance to the Château de Laeken at the Villa Belvedere. The park of Laeken, which became public property at the beginning of the twentieth century, contains a memorial to King Leopold I of the Belgians in the form of a Gothic pyramid. Leopold I and his son Leopold II both died at Laeken and within the grounds of the Château itself there is a memorial cloister to Queen Astrid, the Swedish bride of Leopold III who was killed in a car crash in Switzerland only a year after he succeeded to the throne.

Leopold I (r. 1831–65) had begun life as a fairly impoverished younger son of the Duke of Saxe-Coburg-Saalfeld but then rose to undreamed-of heights by marrying the heiress to the British throne, Princess Charlotte, daughter of George IV. Unfortunately Charlotte died in childbirth, destroying Leopold's chances of becoming the British Prince Consort; after this he became something of a fusspot, wearing a wig to keep his head warm and treble-soled boots to keep out the damp. He considered accepting the throne first of Mexico and then of Greece before satisfying his 'strong liking' for kingship by accepting an offer from the Belgians after they broke away from the Netherlands in 1830.

120 Laeken, Brussels: the residence of King Baudouin and Queen Fabiola in the outskirts of the capital. Originally built from 1782 to 1784 for Princess Marie-Christine of Austria (Governor-General of the Austrian Netherlands) by Montoyer and Payen, the *château* was restored in 1802 and then rebuilt in 1890 after a fire.

121 The Royal Palace, Brussels, which dates from the mid-to-late eighteenth century, was transformed at the beginning of the twentieth century for King Leopold II by Maquet and others. The pediment group by Vincotte shows 'Belgium' between 'Agriculture' and 'Industry'.

The most adroit international politician of his day in Europe, Leopold I shrewdly took a French princess for his second wife and set about establishing Coburg dynasties on the thrones of Britain and Portugal. He also concerned himself with Belgium's industrial advancement. His son and successor eventually provided the new country with a vast colonial territory in central Africa in 1908 which he developed more or less single-handed. This venture brought the tall, long-nosed, long-bearded monarch much wealth but also landed him in trouble on account of the ill-treatment of natives in the Congo. This scandal and his lecherous conduct, which he did not trouble to hide, made Leopold II one of the least attractive European sovereigns of his day. In fairness, however, it must be said that he did spend much of his African fortune on medical research in the Congo and on public works in Belgium.

Ostend was developed as a resort and, though admittedly he preferred his clutch of residences on the Riviera (where he could take the air on a motorcycle), Leopold II maintained a villa here. One English visitor described it as 'a simple enough place', recording that

> One who had business with His Majesty rang the bell. A footman opened the door, took your hat, and led you directly to him in his study, through one or two very ordinary rooms. The only feature that lingers in my memory is the shrill blue velvet with which the furniture was upholstered – an awful colour!

Leopold II's major contribution to the ceremonial aspect of the Belgian monarchy was the lavish rebuilding of the royal palaces in Brussels from 1904 to

1912. Various architects, principally Maquet, took a hand in Leopold's grandiose scheme, drawing their inspiration from Versailles and the Tuileries. Vincotte's group in the pediment shows Belgium strategically positioned between the figures of Agriculture and Industry. The interior features include the Venetian staircase, some famous chandeliers in the Throne Room and Gobelin tapestries in the Grand White Drawing Room, as well as a pair of canopied beds in the short-lived 'Queen Louise' style (Leopold I's wife was the daughter of the French 'Citizen-King' Louis Philippe).

The building, which stands on a slope, has been described as looking like a piece of cake about to slip off a carelessly balanced plate. Part of it is on the site of

122 Het Huis ten Bosch: the Chinese Room. A comparatively late example of eighteenth-century *chinoiserie*, this apartment (and the Japanese Room in the palace) was presented to Prince William V by the head of the Dutch East India Company at Canton in 1791. The furniture was reassembled here in the 1950s.

123 (*above*) The Grand Ducal Palace in the centre of Luxembourg was originally the Town Hall, built by Count Mansfeld in 1572, but was enlarged by Grand Duke Adolphe after he succeeded in 1890. The 'Ruritanian' air is enhanced by the sentry-boxes.

124 (*right*) The *Palais du Roi*, Brussels: the *Salon Rouge*, with portraits of King Leopold I and his French queen, Louise Marie, daughter of the 'Citizen-King' Louis Philippe. She gave her name to the so-called 'Queen Louise' style of decoration.

the old palace of the Dukes of Brabant, burnt down in 1731. This presumably was the place Dürer visited in 1520, describing it as 'very splendidly built and beautifully adorned' with 'two fine large halls and treasures everywhere, also the great bed wherein fifty men can lie'.

The palace is just east of the Rue Royale where King Albert, Leopold II's son, was frequently to be seen in his off-duty moments walking by himself, informally dressed in a tweed suit. His subjects respected his privacy. 'Look, quick!' exclaimed an American excitedly to his Belgian companion. 'Isn't that King Albert? Look!'

'It is King Albert', replied the Belgian. 'That is why I am not looking.'

The popular Albert was killed rock-climbing while still in his prime, and his son Leopold III had a difficult time in the Second World War after surrendering the country to the Germans. Following his father's eventual abdication in 1951, King Baudouin has worked hard at restoring Belgian confidence in the monarchy.

On his visit to Brussels in 1520, Dürer also recorded 'a view most beautiful' which he did not believe 'that in all Germany the like exists' over the 'beast' and pleasure garden. Today the royal palace enjoys a fine view of the park laid out in the late 1770s by Zinner, the Austrian court gardener. Some of the fiercest fighting in the 1830 uprising against the Old Frog, King William I of the Netherlands, took place here.

That other offshoot from the Netherlands, the Grand Duchy of Luxembourg, grew out of the more peaceful soil of the Nassau family pact so that in 1890 when the young Queen Wilhelmina succeeded to the Dutch throne, her father William III's Grand Duchy passed to the senior branch of the House of Nassau. At that stage the Grand Duchy was bound by Salic Law (which banned inheritance through the female line), but this was conveniently altered by family statute so as to enable Grand Duchess Marie Adelaide to succeed in 1912. At the outbreak of the First World War, the 20-year-old Grand Duchess (the first sovereign of Luxembourg to have been born in the Grand Duchy) captured the imagination of her subjects – and indeed of the people of the Allied countries – by driving to the frontier, stopping her motor-car in the way of the invading German army and ordering these gatecrashers out of her country. This spirited, if futile, gesture is recalled by the story of the 'Grand Duchy of Fenwick' in the Peter Sellers film *The Mouse that Roared*.

The Grand Duchy is an area of a thousand square miles and, like Liechtenstein, is living proof that small monarchies are beautiful. The Grand-Ducal Palace was originally built in 1572 as the town hall by the then governor, Count Mansfeld, but was enlarged by Grand Duke Adolphe soon after he succeeded in 1890. The Gothic study of Grand Duke William IV is much as it was in 1912 when he died, though parts of the interior suffered from the palace's occupation during the Second World War by the German army, when it was used as a Nazi officers' club. The paintings of the twelve Luxembourg cantons on the ceiling of the waiting-room, for instance, were whitewashed over. The decoration inside includes tapestries in the dining-room which were a present from Napoleon. Only about 40 people can be squeezed into this room, so when the present Grand Duke, a former officer in the Irish Guards, married King Baudouin's sister in 1953 a passage was knocked into the Chamber of Deputies where the reception was held.

The family homes of the Grand Duke and Duchess are Fischbach and the Château de Colmar-Berg, where the Grand Duke was born. Colmar-Berg was enlarged by Grand Duke Adolphe from an old hunting-lodge into a ponderous turreted pile to the designs of some romantically-minded German architects. The well-laid-out botanic gardens are its best feature. During the Second World War Colmar-Berg was used as a Hitler School for Girls.

The Grand Duke's mother, the redoubtable Grand Duchess Charlotte, succeeded her sister when she abdicated amid the political quagmire of 1919 (Marie Adelaide then became a Carmelite nun but died five years later). On his father's side, the Grand Duke is a Bourbon-Parma; there are thus two reigning Bourbons today, Grand Duke Jean and King Juan Carlos of Spain – more, in fact, than there have been for over a century.

Scandinavia

DENMARK, NORWAY AND SWEDEN

125 (*previous page*) Oslo: the neo-Classical royal palace, built from 1824 to 1848. (*See page 161*)

126 (*left*) Frederiksborg Castle, Northern Zealand: the pinnacle of the 'Danish Renaissance'.

127 (*below*) Kronborg Castle: the chapel. This is the best preserved of the rooms built by Frederick II (from 1577 to 1585), which also suffered a fire in 1629. Consecrated in 1582, the chapel still has its original oak furnishings. The carving of the pews and pulpit was done by Jesper Mathiesen.

The father of the Empress Marie of Russia, Christian IX of Denmark, could not afford to go to St Petersburg for her wedding in 1866 because of the largesse which the Russians would have expected him to contribute. Being the 'Father-in-law of Europe' (his eldest daughter, Alexandra, had married the future Edward VII of Great Britain in 1863) put a severe strain on his finances. He had other problems: in 1864, Denmark had lost half its European territory to Prussia in the Schleswig-Holstein conflict. When the war was going badly, a mob attacked the half-German king's Amalienborg Palace in Copenhagen with shouts of 'Traitor!'

As the unhappy events of 1864 receded, Christian IX (who had begun life as a younger son of an impoverished cadet branch of the royal family), came to be regarded as the father of his people as well as the Father-in-law of Europe. Apart from his daughters, Christian IX's second son William had been King George I of the Hellenes since 1863; and the Danish king came to occupy a particularly honoured place among European monarchs. But if it was beyond his means to pay many visits to his illustrious children, they were constantly visiting their father and mother, for they were a very united family and loved their old home, Fredensborg Castle. The annual family reunions at the Fredensborg, when all the sons and daughters of Christian IX and Queen Louise would be gathered

128 Amalienborg, Copenhagen, where the ceremonial changing of the guard takes place. In the centre of the *Plads* is Jacques Saly's equestrian statue of Frederick V (erected here in 1768); to the left of the picture is the palace, granted by that king in 1750 to General Greve C. F. von Levetzau. The four palaces that form the Amalienborg were designed by the royal architect Nicolai Eigtved; since 1794 all of them have belonged to the Danish royal family. In the background of the picture is the *Frederikskirken*, 'the marble church'.

together under their parents' roof, together with sons- and daughters-in-law, grandchildren and great-grandchildren, became an institution much talked of in royal circles. Because of the Danish royal family's well-known antipathy to Prussia over the Schleswig-Holstein question, and because the king's youngest daughter, Princess Thyra, was married to the Duke of Cumberland (son of the blind king of Hanover who had been dethroned by Prussia after the war in 1866), Fredensborg came to be regarded as a centre of anti-Prussian intrigue. In fact, these gatherings were little more than an occasion for family gossip and simple fun. The Prince of Wales, who was used to more sophisticated entertainments, found them a little trying – particularly after Christian IX had become rather deaf.

Fredensborg was built in the early 1720s for Frederick IV very much as a palace of pleasure. It is still used for entertainments given by the present Danish royal family, who come here every spring and autumn. Various architects

129 (*above*) King Christian IX and Queen Louise of Denmark at Fredensborg.

130 (*above right*) Fredensborg Castle, built as a pleasure palace for Frederick IV from 1721 to 1723. The two corner pavilions were added in 1752 by Nicolai Eigtved. To the left and right of the picture are the inner ends of the octagon of outbuildings.

contributed over the years of building and subsequent enlargement, including Thura, Nicolai Eigtved, Harsdorff and Nicolas-Henri Jardin, who laid out the park running down to the shores of Lake Esrum in 1760. The Italian Baroque sculptures and the formal gardens, with lime avenues framing the parterres, recall a Renaissance villa, though Fredensborg's façade is distinctly Nordic. The dominating feature is the dome. Inside the palace, some 400 rooms are grouped around the great hall (under the cupola), which is noted for its paintings.

Fredensborg Castle should not be confused with Frederiksborg Castle nearby, which is a product of the early seventeenth-century Danish Renaissance. The moated Frederiksborg was erected on the site of an earlier castle (of Frederick II's time) for that great royal builder, Christian IV. Restored after a fire of 1859, it has been the Museum of Natural History since 1877.

Christian IV also rebuilt the historic castle of Kronborg at Elsinore (immortalized by Shakespeare in *Hamlet*) after a fire of 1629 had destroyed the previous castle which was itself principally a sixteenth-century rebuilding. Christian IV, who was something of an amateur architect himself, collaborated in the rebuilding with Hans von Steenwinckel the Younger (son of a master builder employed by Frederick II here in the late sixteenth century). During the seventeenth-century wars with Sweden, Kronborg was sacked by the invaders; from 1785 to 1922 it was in military use but has since been restored. The chapel, which survived the 1629 fire with its Renaissance interior and wood-carvings intact, and the 200-feet-long Knights' Hall are two of the most interesting features. *Hamlet* is still produced from time to time in the castle courtyard; the ghost of Hamlet's father appears in the Flag Battery ('the platform before the castle').

Fires also played their part in the history of Christiansborg Palace in Copenhagen, begun in 1733 by the puritanical Christian VI on the site of an old

131 (*left*) Stockholm: the Pillared Hall in the Royal Palace.

132 (*above*) Drottningholm: the Chinese Pavilion, finished in 1766 for Queen Louisa Ulrika, the wife of King Adolphus Frederick, as a summer retreat – a sort of Swedish 'Petit Trianon' tucked away in the trees. Inside, there is a mingling of French, Rococo and *chinoiserie*. Nearby, in the park of Drottningholm, is the settlement of 'Canton' (built from 1750 to 1760) where craftsmen worked on furniture and carpets for the Chinese Pavilion.

fortress (erected by Bishop Absalon in 1167) which had been a royal residence since the fifteenth century. In 1794 the new Baroque palace was burnt down; only the riding-school survives today. The next building on the site was a neo-Classical palace designed by C. F. Hansen and used particularly by Frederick VII, who ratified the Constitution here in 1849. He scandalized his royal relations by living with a former dancer and milliner, Louise Rasmussen (whom he created Countess Danner); though, in her favour, she did succeed in curbing the king's drinking and other excesses.

Christiansborg was burnt down a second time in 1884, after it had become the home of the new Parliament. Rebuilt this century by Thorvald Jørgensen, Christiansborg was the scene of the proclamation of Queen Margrethe's accession from its royal balcony in 1972. The tall, talented queen broke an

ancient line of alternating Fredericks and Christians which stretched back to 1513; previously Denmark had only male sovereigns and her right of succession was established by a referendum in 1953.

Queen Margrethe's official residence in Copenhagen is the Amalienborg Palace, although she and her family are able to relax at a cottage south of the capital. The Amalienborg is the collective name of the four palaces grouped like a diamond around the Amalienborg Plads (which commemorates yet another burnt building, the seventeenth-century castle named after Frederick III's queen, Sofie Amalie). Queen Margrethe lives in the palace to the right of the entrance to the Plads; next door is her mother, the Dowager Queen Ingrid; the other two palaces are given over to royal reception rooms and a museum of royal treasures and costumes.

Amalienborg is the legacy of Frederick V, upon whose accession in 1746 Denmark entered the Age of the Rococo. Frederick had none of the puritanism of his father, Christian VI; his court became noted for its gaiety, and he encouraged the arts. A new theatre was opened in 1747, with Holberg as its adviser and chief playwright; a Royal Academy of Art was founded in 1754. Having completed his father's palace of Christiansborg, Frederick planned to extend Copenhagen by building an elegant new quarter to be called Frederiksstaden. Much of this ambitious scheme had to be abandoned owing to shortage of money; but among the new buildings which were completed were

133 (*above left*) Kronborg Castle, Elsinore. Originally an early-fifteenth-century fortress built by Eric of Pomerania, it was rebuilt first by Frederick II (between 1574 and 1585) to the designs of Hans van Paescheng and Anthonis van Opbergen; and then again, after a terrible fire in 1629, by Christian IV. On the left of the picture is the 1581 *Kakkelborg* (or King's) Tower, which has remained fairly unchanged since Frederick II's day. The other tower in view is the Trumpeter's Tower, built after the 1629 fire by Steenwinckel and remodelled in 1777 by C. F. Harsdorff.

134 (*above centre*) Christiansborg, Copenhagen. The present building, which houses the Danish Parliament, dates only from the beginning of the twentieth century when it was designed by Thorvald Jørgensoen. The previous palace on the site had been burned down in 1884; a neo-Classical edifice designed in the early nineteenth century by C. F. Hansen, this, in turn, had replaced the Imperial Baroque palace built by Christian VI from 1733 which was destroyed by fire in 1794. Only the Riding School survives of the eighteenth-century building.

135 (*above right*) Amalienborg, Copenhagen: a bird's-eye view of the *Plads* laid out by Frederick V (whose statue is in the middle) to the designs of Nicolai Eigtved from 1749 onwards. The Queen of Denmark lives in the palace on the south-east side of the *Plads*; the Queen Mother is next door and the other two palaces are given over to royal reception rooms and a museum of royal treasures.

the four matching Rococo palaces of Amalienborg, designed by the royal architect, Nicolai Eigtved. They were originally intended for noblemen, but were acquired by the Crown at the end of the century, after Christiansborg had been largely destroyed by fire.

Eigtved submitted the plans for the development of the Amalienborg Plads area in 1749 to Frederick V and in the following year the king presented the sites to four noblemen with the proviso that the façades should correspond exactly to Eigtved's designs. They were left free as regards the interior. Soon the king's close friend and adviser, Adam Moltke til Bregentved (who was of the same family as the Prussian marshal), outshone his three neighbours in his superb interior decoration. The *Riddersalen* (or Baronial Hall) shows the influence of Eigtved's sometime employer François Cuvilliés (whose best work at Nymphenburg, the Amalienburg Pavilion, has virtually the same name); the white panelled walls are decorated with carved and gilt ornaments. J. B. Fossati did the stucco ceiling, Louis Auguste le Clerc the wood carvings; François Boucher painted the pictures above the fireplaces and the doors.

After Eigtved's death in 1754, Jardin designed the neo-Classical dining-hall for Moltke, who had taken up residence shortly before Eigtved died. The dissipated and ultimately insane Christian VII took over Moltke's palace in 1794 and had some remodelling carried out by Harsdorff. An Ionic colonnade was built linking his palace to that of the Crown Prince (later Frederick VI).

Just before Christian IX died, aged 87, in 1906, he had the final satisfaction of seeing his grandson, Prince Carl (brother of King Frederick IX of Denmark who used to conduct the Danish State Orchestra), elected king of Norway.

When Prince Carl had married his first cousin Princess Maud (daughter of the future Edward VII), the British royal family were unimpressed. 'No *money*, they are not going to give him a *house*', lamented the Duchess of Teck. Her sister, the old Grand Duchess of Mecklenburg-Strelitz, was no more impressed when Princess Maud became queen of Norway. 'Too horrible', she wrote, 'for an English Princess to sit upon a Revolutionary Throne!' And she did not approve when her niece and nephew-in-law, the future Queen Mary and King George V, went to Trondheim for the installation of the new Norwegian king and his consort. 'A *revolutionary* Coronation! Such a *farce*', she told her niece, who replied: 'The whole thing seems curious, but we live in very modern days.'

Prince Carl became King Haakon of Norway and lived at the royal palace in Oslo which had been started by King Karl XIV Johan of Sweden in 1825. Norway had been united to Denmark until 1814, when Frederick VI of Denmark ceded it to Sweden from which 'the Revolutionary' state seceded in 1905.

Karl XIV Johan of Sweden was better known as the Gascon sergeant, Jean Baptiste Bernadotte, who became one of Napoleon's most independent-minded marshals. By an extraordinary twist of fate he was chosen by the Swedes (whom he had defeated in Pomerania in 1807) as Crown Prince in 1810 to the last Swedish king of the Holstein-Gottorp dynasty, the elderly and childless Charles XIII. The Swedes had warmed to their chivalrous and conciliatory conqueror, whose views about Napoleon seemed to coincide with their own. He officially succeeded to the Swedish throne in 1818, having already been the *de facto* sovereign since about 1811.

The commission to design the new Norwegian royal palace was entrusted by Karl XIV Johan to H. D. F. Linstow. The architect's first plan was for a vast H-shaped three-storeyed central block with lower wings built at right-angles. But the palace was altered and reduced so many times before it was completed in 1847 that it ended up as a much simpler affair. None the less it certainly creates a monumental effect, with its portico and columns, at the top of the hill leading down to Karl Johan's Gate in the town's centre. The interior has suitably regal state apartments, including two ballrooms. King Olav of Norway, the symbol of 'Free Norway' in the Second World War and a man of the sea like his father King Haakon, lives at Bygdöy near the yachting centre of Hankö in the summer and also has a mountain retreat. The king began his education in the royal palace, but in 1913 started attending the Halling School, thus becoming the first prince in the world to attend a grammar school.

Bernadotte's son, Oscar I of Sweden, pursued the ideal of a united Scandinavia, working hard to tie Sweden and Norway closely to Denmark; but he died in 1859 with his dream of a Scandinavian 'great power' unrealized. About five years before his death, Oscar I was threatened with blindness. He was cured by an eminent Irish oculist, who would accept no fee for his services. When the king asked if he could reward him in any other way, the doctor said

137 Skaugum, Oslofjord: the smoking-room. This is the residence of the Crown Prince of Norway, Harald, the Olympic yachtsman. It was given to him by his father, King Olav, as a wedding present.

that he had just heard that his wife, whom he had left behind in Dublin, had given birth to a son, and that he would be much honoured if the king would be the child's godfather. Oscar I willingly consented, and the child was duly given his name. The godson was destined to be more famous than the godfather, for the doctor was Sir William Wilde.

Bernadotte, or rather Karl XIV Johan, must have felt at home in the very French royal palace on the waterside at Stockholm, which was built off and on between 1697 and 1754 when the first Swedish king of the Holstein-Gottorp dynasty, Adolphus Frederick, moved in. One courtier said of his former Prince-Bishop of Lübeck that he 'looked gracious even from behind'. Adolphus Frederick died suddenly at the royal palace following a supper of buns, sauerkraut, oysters, lobster and champagne.

The old Three Crowns palace of the Vasa line (which included the great seventeenth-century soldier Gustavus Adolphus and his daughter Queen Christina) was burnt down in May 1697; and the very next day Nicodemus

138 Stockholm: a waterside view of the largest of the Scandinavian royal palaces. Built from 1697 to 1754 to the designs of the Tessin architectural dynasty, the royal palace showed southern inspiration and yet is also firmly Swedish.

Tessin the Younger came up with a plan for a new palace. Tessin had been inspired by his travels around Europe; his design for the exterior was influenced by the Italian late Renaissance and Baroque, but inside it was – as one American lady put it in another context – 'so Louis it was *Louis Louis*'. A team of French artists and craftsmen embellished the interior, including the sculptor Réné Chauveau and the silversmith Jean-François Cousinet.

Work was suspended on the new royal palace at Stockholm in 1710 after Charles XII's martial deeds had bankrupted Sweden. Poor Tessin had to wait another eighteen years before building was resumed and then he promptly died. However, his son Carl Gustav Tessin followed in his father's footsteps with the help of the family protégé Carl Hårleman. Together they augmented the French decoration with tremendous enthusiasm, adding rich collections of Boucher tapestries (Tessin dallied with Mme Boucher during his spell as Swedish envoy to the French court), Savonnerie carpets, furniture and *objets d'art*. The furnishings that were not imported were principally the work of another

Francophile Swede, Jean Eric Rehn, who was also kept busy at the other royal residences.

In keeping with its progressive character Sweden can boast that the royal palace in Stockholm is supremely accessible. The young king, Carl XVI Gustaf, can step out of his front door on to one of the busiest streets in the capital and passers-by can step in to survey some of the 550 rooms – such as the Hall of State, with the silver throne; the Chapel Royal, with its pews saved from the old palace; and the opulently Frenchified guest apartments.

Nicodemus Tessin the Elder has a place in Swedish architectural history for his design of Drottningholm, the so-called 'Versailles of the North', a charming but very Nordic country house on an island in Lake Malar. Tessin the Younger

139 Drottningholm, 'the Versailles of the North'. Built in 1662 for Queen Eleanora to the designs of Nicodemus Tessin the Elder, the palace is still the home of the present king and queen of Sweden. Tessin's son and namesake laid out the gardens in the style of Le Nôtre. Queen Louisa Ulrika of Sweden (a sister of Frederick the Great of Prussia) was given Drottningholm as a wedding present in 1744 and added new wings by Carl Härleman and Carl Fredrik Adelcrantz.

140 (*above right*) Drottningholm: Adelcrantz's theatre of 1766 with the eighteenth-century scenery still intact. Following the death of that great patron of the arts, Gustavus III, in 1792, the theatre was neglected until this century. Now once again Baroque operas are performed here.

also worked at Drottningholm, taking an active interest in the completion of the formal gardens along the familiar Le Nôtre lines. The grounds of this summer palace contain its best features: the China Palace tucked away in the trees as a sort of Trianon, and the delightful theatre forever associated with Gustavus III, the patron of the arts who presided over Sweden's Golden Age in the late eighteenth century.

After he was mortally wounded by an assassin at a masked ball in the Royal Theatre in Stockholm (an event on which Verdi based his opera *Un Ballo in Maschera*), the theatre at Drottningholm fell into disuse. The original scenery, props and other paraphernalia, however, remained *in situ*. Then, after a hundred or so years, like the Sleeping Beauty, the boarded-up theatre yielded its secrets to a student searching for documents. The cobwebs were brushed away to reveal the eighteenth-century stage machinery still in perfect working order. And so, once more, the auditorium is today filled with the sounds of Baroque opera.

Gustavus III, who so relished those magical sounds, acquired another Swedish country house for the Holstein-Gottorp dynasty, at Tullgarn on an inlet from the Baltic, in 1772. The previous owners were the de la Gardie family who had built the Baroque villa some fifty years earlier to the designs of Joseph-Gabriel Destain, influenced by Tessin. Gustavus III put Tullgarn at the disposal of his younger brother, Duke Fredrik of Östergötland, a bachelor with Italian leanings, who proceeded to redecorate the interior in the neo-Classical style. The principal author of the decorative work was Jean-Baptiste Masreliez; one of his assistants, the painter Anders Hultgren, enlivened the decorations by his naturalistic interpretations among the staid Classicism.

Tullgarn has not featured among the residences used by the Swedish royal family since the death of the redoubtable Gustaf V Adolf in 1950. This king, who was still to be seen on the tennis court in his eighties, had moved here after his marriage in 1881 to Princess Victoria of Baden and had refurbished the place in the 'German *bierstube* renaissance' style, topped up with quantities of Swedish peasant art.

Gustaf V Adolf's great-grandson, Carl XVI Gustaf, who succeeded him only 23 years later, receives a special grant from the Swedish Government to maintain the furnishings in the royal palaces at Stockholm and Drottningholm which both belong to the nation. He also has the use of Stenhammar in Södermanland, while personally owning the summer retreat of Solliden on the Island of Oland (off the east coast of Sweden), which was built by his mother Princess Sybilla. Carl Gustaf is the head of state but is not allowed any political influence; he has to pay income, wealth and property tax and duties on tobacco and alcohol.

Italy and the Two Sicilies

141 (*previous page*) The long façade of Caserta, designed by Luigi Vanvitelli for Charles III. Begun in 1752, it was finished by the architect's son, Carlo, after Luigi's death in 1773. (*See pages 176, 178*)

142 The Quirinal, Rome. The Renaissance entrance front was designed by Flaminio Ponzio and Carlo Maderno with a doorway by Bernini. Begun in 1547 as a summer residence for the Popes, it became the Roman palace of the kings of Italy in 1870.

Early in 1861, Victor Emmanuel II of Savoy, King of Piedmont-Sardinia, proclaimed himself 'King of Italy', not just by the Grace of God, but 'by the Will of the Nation'. Such a rider befitted a king who owed his new unified kingdom, in part at least, to the forces of revolution. The *Risorgimento* of Italy owed something to Garibaldi and his 'Thousand', to Napoleon III (Victor Emmanuel's ally in the war against the Austrians), and almost everything to Camillo Cavour, the cunning politician totally dedicated to the unification of the various Italian states under the House of Savoy.

In 1870 Pope Pio Nono became the 'Prisoner in the Vatican' and Victor Emmanuel II made a triumphal entry into the Eternal City. In common with other triumphs of the ever-acquisitive House of Savoy, this was rather an anticlimax: it is said that he was welcomed at the gates of the city by twenty people.

Victor Emmanuel II took up residence in the papal palace of the Quirinal, though without much enthusiasm, having been told by a fortune-teller that he would die there. His time at the palace did not begin auspiciously, for the Pope refused to hand over the keys so that the Quirinal had to be broken into. Victor Emmanuel II's court was also boycotted by the grandees of the 'Black' nobility. In 1878 the fortune-teller's prophecy came true when Victor Emmanuel II was struck down unexpectedly by pneumonia at the age of 57. When Pio Nono heard that this king, from whom he had suffered so much, was dying, he sent his own chaplain to give him the comfort of the Last Sacraments.

The Quirinal was originally envisaged as a summer residence for the popes and building work began in 1547. By 1592, however, Pope Clement VIII had already decamped from the unhealthy Vatican to live here all the year round. The fine site had been chosen in the first instance by Cardinal Ippolito d'Este for his town palace and gardens. The present building was started under the direction of the architect Flaminio Ponzio and he was followed by a procession of illustrious artists such as Domenico Fontana, Carlo Maderno, Bernini and Fuga.

The Renaissance façade by Maderno is cheered up by a door designed by the great Bernini. The tower was added in the early seventeenth century. The kings of Italy (and, since 1947, the presidents) lived in the more intimate part of the palace, the *palazzetto*, at the far end of the long wing overlooking the Via del Quirinale. This wing, known as the *manica lunga* (the 'long sleeve'), is where the cardinals used to camp out during papal elections. Before the arrival of Victor Emmanuel II in 1870, the conclaves were held in the *Cappella Paolina* which was built along the same lines as the Sistine Chapel and consecrated in 1611. The chapel is noted for its frescoes by Michelangelo. Other special features of the Quirinal include the fragment from the church of SS. Apostoli of Melozzo da Forlì's fresco of the *Last Judgement* on the grand staircase; a hall of mirrors, with Murano glass chandeliers; and a *chinoiserie* salon.

Before they reached the supreme heights of the Quirinal, the House of Savoy's principal palace was in the centre of Turin. Victor Amadeus I, Duke of Savoy, decided to build a palace here in the 1630s, though little movement was made until 1646 when his widow (known as *Madama Reale*), who was then acting as Regent, brought in Amedeo di Castellamonte. By 1663, the long main block of

143 The Quirinal: the Sala Regia, which was designed by Maderno for Pope Paul V in the early seventeenth century. The frieze was supervised by Agostino Tassi, with figures by Lanfranco and Carlo Saraceni. Above the relief of Christ washing St Peter's feet by Taddeo Landini are the papal arms supported by statues – the work of Berthelot and Bernini.

the façade, as well as most of the east wing (now the Armoury), were finished. In 1666 Charles Emmanuel II commissioned Guarino Guarini to complete Castellamonte's chapel which the Duke wanted to house his dynasty's most famous possession, the sacred relic of the Holy Shroud. At the same time he wanted Guarini to provide a stately link between the cathedral and the royal palace, which is on a lower level. Guarini's dome over the *Cappella della Santa Sidone* is a masterpiece, appearing, as James Lees-Milne has said, 'like a glimmering star whose pointed rays issue from the Holy Ghost in a blaze of glory'. The precision of Guarini's work suggests to Lees-Milne 'the carefully laid twigs of a bird's nest'.

Various hands contributed to the embellishment of the palace at Turin which carried on through the eighteenth century, as the House of Savoy expanded its territories, right up to the time of Charles Albert (King of Sardinia from 1831), who indulged in some neo-Classical decorative touches here.

Daniele Seiter, in Turin from 1688 to 1705, executed numerous ceiling paintings. Filippo Juvarra, the greatest Italian designer of the eighteenth century, who became 'First Architect' to Victor Amadeus II in 1714, was responsible for the Scissor Staircase and the outstanding Chinese Room. Below a coved ceiling filled with a painting of *The Judgement of Paris* by Claudio Beaumont are black and gold lacquer panels, silver mirrors, red and gold walls and scrollwork by Angelo Sariga and Vietto. The Mirror Room is by Count Benedetto Alfieri, who succeeded Juvarra in 1736, and features miniatures of the House of Savoy by Giuseppe Nogari. The mid-nineteenth-century touches of royal purple and gold in other parts of the palace were supplied by the Bolognese Pelagio Palagi; the Alcove Room (where Charles Emmanuel II used to sleep) is an explosion of gilt. Finally, in 1864, Victor Emmanuel II added the marble staircase by Augusto Ferri with its life-size statues of this ambitious dynasty.

144 (*above left*) Turin: the royal palace, from the garden. It was designed by Amedeo di Castellamonte in the eighteenth century.

145 (*above centre*) Stupinigi, near Turin: the Great Saloon. The astonishing scale of Juvarra's work here in this central oval saloon recalls Versailles, while his dramatic treatment has been compared to Borromini's. The decorations are by the brothers Valeriani.

146 (*above right*) Turin: the Armoury of the 1660s,
in the east wing.

The House of Savoy's 'Versailles' outside Turin was the Palazzo Stupinigi, built in the early eighteenth century for Victor Amadeus II. This Duke of Savoy became an international joke on account of the number of times that he changed sides: he alternated with dizzying frequency between fighting for and against his cousin, Louis XIV. Stupinigi began as a modest hunting-box but then grew under the inspired hand of Juvarra into a superb Baroque palace. Inside are a series of marvellous apartments of varying shapes and a quantity of painted decoration. The central saloon is the high-point with a dome, vaults, walls and piers painted by the brothers Valeriani with emblems of the chase. The original chandelier and furnishings make this saloon one of the most magnificent in Europe. Stupinigi is also remembered because Napoleon stayed here in 1805 on his way to Milan, where he was crowned King of Italy.

It is unfortunate that the House of Savoy now tends to be associated in the mind's eye with unappealing public buildings such as the gargantuan white marble Victor Emmanuel II Monument in Rome, which expressed the grandiose schemes of empire in the late nineteenth and early twentieth centuries, rather than with, say, the delights of Stupinigi. For sheer size and pomposity these erections of the 'bourgeois monarchy' outdo even the monuments of the German Reich and are in painful contrast with the elegance and natural good taste of the Italian architecture of every previous age.

The Bourbon Kingdom of the Two Sicilies, which the House of Savoy swallowed in 1861, is, on the other hand, forever associated with Neapolitan

147 Naples, royal palace: the bay façade.

glory. 'Dear Naples will be more beautiful than ever!' the people are said to have exclaimed when King Charles entered his capital in 1734, and their new sovereign did not disappoint them. From 1504 to 1707, the ancient kingdom of Naples or the Two Sicilies belonged to Spain, and was governed by Spanish viceroys. Having been acquired by Austria during the War of the Spanish Succession, it was conquered in 1734 by this 18-year-old Bourbon, son of Philip V of Spain.

Instead of spending his money on wars, Charles spent it on beautifying his kingdom. His own interests were sporting rather than artistic or scholarly. And yet he built Caserta and other glorious palaces; he started the famous Capodimonte porcelain factory (which vied with Augustus of Saxony's factory at Meissen); he sponsored the excavations of Herculaneum and Pompeii. In Naples itself his buildings included the original San Carlo Theatre and a vast 'palace for the poor', the Reale Albergo dei Poveri. The wealthier nobles emulated him and built themselves new palaces or embellished their existing ones so that during the course of Charles's reign Naples was transformed into one of the finest capitals in Europe. Soon it was known as the 'Metropolis of Italy'. As well as its wealth and grandeur, and its traditional reputation for music, it became famous, under Charles and his successor, as a centre of science, scholarship and advanced thought. In the words of Sir Harold Acton, 'Charles had brought with him a salutary breeze of optimism, an intellectual freedom which was luminous in comparison with other Italian states'.

148 Naples, royal palace: the double-flighted marble staircase. Originally designed by Domenico Fontana, the work was carried out by F. A. Picchiati in 1651 but later altered by Gaetano Genovese after a fire in 1837.

Charles wasted no time in extending the royal palace at Naples, adding the wing along the sea front to house his collection of incunabula and manuscripts which formed the nucleus of the National Library. Count Lemos, the Spanish viceroy, had built the palace at the start of the seventeenth century to the designs of Domenico Fontana, who had become the 'Royal Engineer' in Naples after falling out of favour in Rome. The original façade differed a little from what we see today. The present roofing is higher and each alternate arch of the portico has been filled in (on the advice of Luigi Vanvitelli in the eighteenth century) to form a series of niches – these now contain statues of Neapolitan rulers. Inside, the impressive double-flighted marble staircase was put up in 1651 by F. A. Picchiati to Fontana's original design, although this was later altered by Gaetano Genovese when he renovated the palace after a fire in 1837.

149 (*left*) Caserta: the shadowy giant of the palace as it appears from the top of the cascade. Luigi Vanvitelli had the water channelled from Monte Taburno some 25 miles away; the cascade draws its supply for the inexorable journey to the palace from the Carolina Aqueduct.

150 (*right*) Caserta: at the foot of the cascade is the Diana and Actaeon tableau of statues, variously attributed.

In 1738 the Sicilian architect G. A. Medrano was responsible for the design of the pinkish Capodimonte Palace, set in an attractive park which also contained the famous porcelain works. Originally King Charles had envisaged a hunting-lodge but then decided to call on Medrano to build him a palace large enough to house the great collection of art treasures he had inherited from his mother, Elisabeth Farnese. The present building at Capodimonte was not in fact completed until a hundred years later when it became one of the principal residences of 'King Bomba', otherwise Ferdinand II. Today Capodimonte is a museum and picture gallery.

In the same year that he started Capodimonte, Charles visited the villa of the Prince of Elboeuf at Portici in the foothills of Vesuvius and was so struck by the beauty of the site that he promptly commissioned the faithful Medrano to design the *Palazzo Reale* here. Charles's courtiers were alarmed at the proposed palace's proximity to the volcanic mountain, but the king made light of the danger: 'God, Mary Immaculate and San Gennaro will see to that.' To be on the safe side, however, he did check with the Neapolitan scientists whose prognostication that the lava flows would not reach the palace has been proved correct.

Charles's palace at Portici is built round an octagonal courtyard-piazza. Some of the state rooms inside were done over when Joachim Murat was ruling Naples as a satellite kingdom of Napoleon ('The dynasty of Naples has ceased to reign', trumpeted the latter in 1806). Since the Bourbons finally did cease to reign in 1860 the *Palazzo Reale* has been an agricultural college.

In 1752 Charles began building his most ambitious palace, Caserta, the Versailles of the Kingdom of the Two Sicilies. He had confiscated the estate of the disaffected Prince of Sermoneta (later paid 489,348 ducats to keep him quiet) in the Terra di Lavoro with a view to creating a new administrative capital for the kingdom. But the grandiloquent plans for blocks of offices were not carried out and Caserta ended up as more of a summer palace. The architect Luigi Vanvitelli worked away here until his death in 1773 and the enormous exterior was finally concluded by his son Carlo.

The long, rather monotonous front badly misses the swaggering touches of the original design which included a central cupola. However, as built, the façade is framed by projecting pillared pavilions at either end and in the centre a pediment surmounts two arches. Inside, the main doorway leads to a vast atrium which in turn heralds an astonishing vista stretching out to the lawns, water and the cascade in the hillside two miles away.

With a command of nature comparable to that demonstrated at Versailles, Vanvitelli had all this water channelled in from Monte Taburno some 25 miles away, across five mountains and three valleys. Along the sinister avenue of water leading to the dramatic cascade are sculptured groups, such as Diana and Actaeon, by artists including Tommaso Solari, Paolo Persico, Andrea Violani, Gaetano Salamoni and Andrea Brunelli.

King Bomba's seven-year-old son was once lost for over an hour inside Caserta. Certainly a tour of this palace eventually becomes overwhelming. Among the finest rooms are the Halberdiers' Hall, with its sculpture of Victory crowning Alexander Farnese; the theatre, with its green marble columns from

151 (*above*) Stupinigi: a lavishly decorated apartment devoted to the pleasures of the chase. The paintings are by Cignaroli and others.

152 (*right*) Turin, royal palace: the Chinese Room designed by Filippo Juvarra, who became 'First Architect' to Victor Amadeus II of Savoy in 1714. The scrollwork was carved by Angelo Sariga and Vietto. The ceiling painting of the *Judgment of Paris* is by Claudio Beaumont.

153 Capodimonte: the principal façade. Designed by the Sicilian architect G. A. Medrano in 1738 for Charles III, the palace was completed a century later for Ferdinand II.

the Temple of Serapis at Pozzuoli; the Throne Room, decorated in 1845 for King Bomba by Angelini, Tommaso Arnoud and Genovese. The bathrooms relieve the monotony; one early example of stylish Pompeian plumbing has a gilded bath and a gold tap, while in the nineteenth-century apartments there is a stone bath adorned with lions' heads complemented by an alabaster dressing-table with a fountain for scent in its middle.

Caserta had only risen as far as the first storey when Charles succeeded to the Spanish throne in 1759. As Charles II of Spain, he was to be the most successful Spanish monarch since Philip II; historians tend to regard his years on the throne of Naples as merely an apprenticeship for the real task of his life. On departing from Naples, he took with him the craftsmen from the Capodimonte factory; but he scrupulously left behind all his works of art and other objects of value, regarding them as 'the patrimony of the state' – even the Farnese pictures which he had brought from Parma and a ring which he had found in the diggings at Pompeii.

Charles was succeeded as king of Naples by his third son, Ferdinand, his eldest son being feeble-minded, and the second being destined to rule Spain. At the time of his father's departure, Ferdinand was only eight, and he was left under the regency of Charles's otherwise able minister, Bernardo Tanucci, who unfortunately completely neglected the education of the young king. He grew up almost illiterate, making his friends among the lower palace servants, the gamekeepers and the beaters. As he spoke the dialect of these *lazzaroni*, he came to be known as the 'Lazzarone King'. His only interests were shooting, for which he conceived an even greater passion than his father, and sea-fishing. On returning from a successful fishing expedition, he would himself auction his catch in the fish-market, to the accompaniment of much cheerful banter; and having obtained the highest possible price for it, he would give the money to the poor.

In appearance, Ferdinand was tall, gaunt and gangling, with a good-natured but complacent smile and a huge nose which won him his popular nickname of 'Nasone'. 'Although an ugly Prince, he is not absolutely repulsive', his brother-in-law, the Emperor Joseph II, wrote of him. 'He is clean except for his hands; and at least he does not stink.' This partial cleanliness seems to have been Ferdinand's only refinement; in other respects, his coarseness was proverbial. At court festivities, he would indulge in boisterous and juvenile horseplay, slapping the ladies' buttocks, kicking those of the gentlemen, shouting obscenities and vulgar jokes at the top of his high-pitched voice. He would make his courtiers stand round him and amuse him with their conversation while he sat on his *chaise-percée*. Admittedly this had also been the custom of his most illustrious forebear, Louis XIV; but manners had changed since then. When asked how he liked his bride, the Archduchess Maria Carolina, daughter of Maria Theresa, he replied: '*Suda come un porco*' ('sweats like a pig'). When standing on the palace balcony with his exalted, correct and extremely well-brought-up brother-in-law, the Emperor Joseph, who was paying him a visit, 'he made a very unwarrantable noise', excusing himself by saying that it was necessary for his health: '*E necessario per la salute, fratello mio!*'

154 (*above*) Stupinigi. The hunting-box of Victor Amadeus II of Savoy was transformed by his architect Filippo Juvarra into a Baroque palace between 1729 and 1731.

155 (*left*) Caserta: the bedroom of Francis II, the last king of the Two Sicilies, who lost his throne when his kingdom was annexed to the new Kingdom of Italy in 1861. The Pompeian frieze is a characteristic piece of decoration at Caserta.

156 (*right*) Caserta: the Throne Room, which was decorated in 1845 for Ferdinand II of the Two Sicilies ('King Bomba') by Angelini, Tommaso Arnaud and Genovese. The painting on the ceiling depicts Charles III laying the foundation stone of the vast palace in 1752.

Impossible and incorrigible though he may have been, there was nevertheless something likeable about Ferdinand. Though selfish, he genuinely wanted his subjects to be happy; his indolence and neglect of his kingly duties made him a tolerant, easy-going monarch entirely suited to the Neapolitan temperament. He was a complete Neapolitan himself, as were the later members of his dynasty, the Bourbons of Naples being, like their Spanish cousins, a notable example of environment over heredity.

Spain and Portugal

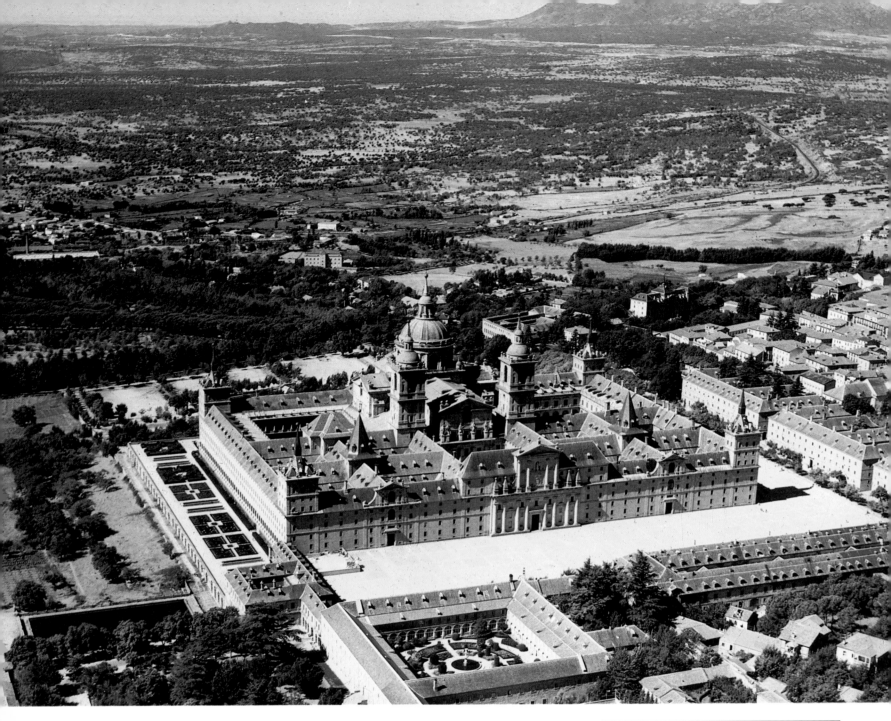

157 (*previous page*) The vast convent-palace of Mafra, built for João V by Frederico Ludovice (formerly Ludwig) from 1717 to 1730. It was the extravagant Portuguese king's attempt to emulate the Escorial. (*See pages 198, 201*)

158 (*above*) The Escorial, near Madrid: the guidelines set by its builder, Philip II of Spain, were simplicity and severity. The 'gridiron' plan recalled St Lawrence's martyrdom. At once a monastery, a cathedral and a palace, the Escorial was built between 1562 and 1584 by the architects Juan Bautista de Toledo and later Juan de Herrera.

159 (*left*) Philip II's rooms in the Escorial reflect his monastic way of life. He died of pediculosis here in 1598, in the bedroom which leads into the Basilica. The pictures include *The Presentation of the Virgin in the Temple* (centre; Flemish School).

160 (*right*) The Alhambra, Granada: the Court of
the Lions, which was begun in 1377 by the Caliph
Mohammed V. There are 124 alabaster columns
in this most famous of the courtyards in the
Moorish palace that so enraptured the Emperor
Charles V.

161 Casita del Labrador is a little villa built close
to the main palace of Aranjuez. Here in this
Spanish *Petit Trianon* is the *Salón Comedor* (or
dining-room). The 93 pictures featured in the
tapestries show various views, including the
Escorial and Aranjuez itself. The 'Four Seasons'
ceiling decoration of 1798 is by Salvador Maella.

As well as being King of Spain, that great sixteenth-century monarch Philip II was also briefly King of England (reigning with his second wife, Mary I) and later King of Portugal for good measure. He inherited the Portuguese crown from his mother's brother, the Cardinal-King Henry, in 1580—or, to put it another way, he annexed the country—and for the next sixty years the Crowns of Portugal and Spain were united.

Philip II dedicated himself to his religion and to the arts; the two were combined in that amazing building outside Madrid, the Escorial, otherwise known as the 'Royal Monastery of St Lawrence'. It was on St Lawrence's day in 1557 that Philip II heard the news of the victory over the French at St Quentin and vowed to build a monastery dedicated to the Spanish martyr. The idea was that the monastery would be served by monks of the Hieronymite Order in whose convent at Yuste his father, the Emperor Charles V, had died. The monastery would also incorporate a royal palace in which the king would live and a mausoleum in which he would be buried.

The mausoleum was not in fact built until the next century; but the rest of the incredible project (1,200 doors, 2,600 windows, 12 courtyards, 86 staircases and 1,500 workmen) was accomplished between 1562 and 1584 under the obsessive supervision of the king himself. The ground plan was by Juan Bautista de Toledo, who had worked under Michelangelo on St Peter's; after his death in 1567 Juan de Herrera took over. 'Simplicity in the construction, severity in the whole, nobility without arrogance, majesty without ostentation' were the guidelines set by Philip II.

The king was determined to avoid unnecessary ornament. The building's 'gridiron' plan was designed to recall St Lawrence's martyrdom by roasting. The grey granite used was meant to emphasize the austerity of the architecture. However, when the king decided he needed more height to accommodate a larger religious community, Herrera took the opportunity offered by the extension to place the endless rows of windows asymmetrically. This served to lessen the monotonous effect of horizontal lines which, otherwise, is only relieved by the pointed corner towers.

By the time the exterior of the Escorial was completed Philip II had fourteen years of his life left to decorate the interior. Most of the rooms in the palace are surprisingly small, save for the Throne Room and the Hall of the Ambassadors. But there is much to see in the way of pictures (such as El Greco's *Dream of Philip II* and *Martyrdom of St Maurice* in the Sala Capitular); manuscripts (in the vaulted library with a ceiling frescoed by Pellegrino Tibaldi and Bartolome Carducho); *objets d'art* such as Benvenuto Cellini's crucifix. However, Philip II's proudest possession, a feather from the wing of the Archangel Gabriel (described by the English collector and traveller William Beckford as 'full three foot long, and of a blushing hue more soft and delicate than that of the loveliest rose'), is, alas, no longer available for the public gaze.

Philip II slept in an austere alcove overlooking the high altar of the Basilica and it was here that he died a terrible death from pediculosis in 1598. For seven weeks he was consumed by body lice, the only relief coming from the sound of mass being sung below.

162 Aranjuez, near Madrid. Following three fires (1660, 1665 and finally 1748), the palace was remodelled by Ferdinand VI to the Rococo designs of Santiago Bonavia from Piacenza. Two wings were added in the 1770s by Francesco Sabatini, son-in-law of Luigi Vanvitelli (the builder of Caserta).

During the wedding tour of Philip II's parents, the Emperor Charles V and his Portuguese wife, they stayed at the old Moorish palace of the Alhambra, overlooking Granada, which had finally capitulated to the Catholic Monarchs in 1492. The emperor was so enchanted by this magical place that he commissioned Pedro Machucha, another former pupil of Michelangelo's, to build a royal residence in the Renaissance style alongside the Moorish masterpiece. Part palace, part harem, the Alhambra consists of a series of exquisite courtyards. The most famous, the Court of the Lions, with its 124 fragile alabaster columns, was begun in 1377 by the Caliph Mohammed V.

The royal palace at Aranjuez on the banks of the River Tagus was originally a hunting-lodge built by Charles V; but his son enlarged it to the designs of Toledo and Herrera, the architects of the Escorial. Two fires in the 1660s abolished most of this, although the English elms planted by Philip II, who took a special interest in the garden here, remain an attractive feature of the surroundings. Aranjuez was then restored by Pedro Caro Idrogo, the overseer of works to Philip V, Louis XIV's grandson, who succeeded to the Spanish throne in 1700. The death of Charles II ('the Bewitched') in that year had brought the Spanish Habsburg line to an end.

163 (*left*) Sintra. The Moorish palace, with its distinctive chimneys, is best seen from below. It was established as a Portuguese royal residence early in the fifteenth century.

165 (*right*) Queluz: *Sala das Merendas*. The jolly 'picnic' room takes its name from the canvases of a *fête champêtre* by João Valentim.

164 (*left*) Queluz: the Music Room. This oval chamber was built in 1759 but redesigned in 1768.

166 (*right*) The charmingly Rococo Queluz is many people's favourite royal palace. Designed by Mateus Vicente and the Frenchman, Jean Baptiste Robillon, who laid out the gardens, it was built from 1758 as a country retreat for Dom Pedro, a younger son of João V of Portugal.

167 San Ildefonso, La Granja: the 'Spanish Versailles'. Built for Philip V from 1719 to 1723 to the designs of Theodore Ardemans, this mountain-top palace was remodelled by Filippo Juvarra from 1735. After Juvarra's death a year later, Juan Battista Sacchetti completed the job.

Philip V was a melancholic and later in life suffered a kind of premature senility. His movements were slow and tremulous, he had a drawling speech and vacant look; he dressed shabbily and had other eccentric habits such as turning night into day and keeping his rooms closely shuttered. His piety verged on religious mania; he would confess twice a day, and have his confessors always at hand to help him in his struggles with his conscience.

Philip suffered most through being over-sexed. After the death of his first wife, he became more melancholy than ever, for his conscience did not permit him to assuage his powerful lusts outside holy wedlock. It was a wonderful relief both to himself and his courtiers when he married again; and so fond was he of his second wife that she was almost always at his side. She was the clever, high-spirited and extremely Italian Elisabeth Farnese, niece of the Duke of Parma.

As a means of relieving Philip V's melancholia the *castrato* Farinelli would sing the same four arias every day to the king. Music was heard again at Aranjuez in the time of Philip V's son, Ferdinand VI, the patron of the composer Domenico Scarlatti, who added a theatre here (with a ceiling by Raphael Mengs) where Italian opera was frequently performed. Indeed the present pinkish appearance of Aranjuez is due to Ferdinand VI who remodelled the building after a third fire (in 1748) to the Rococo designs of Santiago Bonavia from Piacenza, one of the many foreign artists introduced to Spain by Elisabeth Farnese. Two wings were added in the 1770s by Francesco Sabatini, son-in-law of Vanvitelli (the builder of Caserta).

Inside, Aranjuez is more mixed. Outstanding interiors include the Porcelain Room, decorated with plaques from the Buen Retiro factory (which Charles III set up with workmen brought from his former domain at Capodimonte); and the Dining-Room with its paintings by another Neapolitan, Corrado Giaquinto, and a ceiling fresco by Jacopo Amigoni. The chapel frescoes are by Goya's brother-in-law Francisco Bayeu.

In 1724 Philip V surprised everyone by stepping down in favour of his son, Luis, and retired to his new mountain retreat of La Granja de San Ildefonso. Luis, however, died after a reign of eight months, which came as something of a relief to the Spanish courtiers. They had already seen too much of Luis's queen, a sulky hoydenish girl who would run out of doors in an open dressing-gown and hoist her skirts up to her thighs in public.

La Granja is one of the most attractive of all Spanish royal palaces, evoking echoes of Versailles in a superb mountainous setting hewn out of the rock. Philip V's first effort here, however, was rather a gloomy fortress to the design of Theodore Ardemans, built from 1719 to 1723. But in 1735 the king commissioned the great Italian architect Filippo Juvarra to remodel La Granja into a sort of Spanish Baroque version of his grandfather Louis XIV's palace. Juvarra, and later Juan Bautista Sacchetti, naturally favoured the Italianate style, producing a white and pink façade with giant pilasters and Baroque sculptured decoration. The interior witnessed a rich combination of Bourbon and Farnese taste far removed from the sober stateliness of the Habsburgs.

Elisabeth Farnese's influence was also strongly felt in the gardens at La Granja laid out by the Frenchman Boutelon between 1727 and 1743. She was

168 Pena, near Sintra. This extraordinary Manoeline concoction was built for the consort of Queen Maria da Glória of Portugal, Ferdinand of Saxe-Coburg, in the 1840s. The architect was his fellow German, Baron Eschwege. Perched high on a mountain peak, the toy castle enjoys excellent views.

responsible for the Baroque bronze fountains and the cascades served by an artificial lake 200 feet above the palace. Philip V was apparently not best pleased at her extravagance on this occasion. While watching the Baths of Diana in full flow he is said to have remarked: 'It has cost three millions and amused me for three minutes!'

After his son Luis's untimely demise, Philip V came out of his retirement at La Granja and took up the reins of monarchy again until his own death in 1746. His next major building project was the rebuilding of the Oriente Palace in Madrid, which had been burnt down on Christmas Eve 1734. The old palace on the site of the Moorish Alcazar (partially destroyed by an earthquake in 1466) had been enlarged over the centuries by, among others, the Emperor Charles V and Philip II. Philip V commissioned Juvarra to design an enormous edifice of the composite order with four façades (each 1,700 feet long) and 23 inner courts (approached by 34 entrances). After Juvarra's death in 1736, Sacchetti reduced these fantastic plans to reality and building work began in 1738. Philip V died long before it was finished.

The exterior of the Oriente, with its pediment, portico and balustrade, is imposing but the principal splendours lie within. The *Sala de Gasparini* has a polychrome stucco *chinoiserie* ceiling; while the neo-Classical *Sala de Porcelana* contains another of Charles III's arrangements of porcelain plaques. By contrast, among the sixty-odd apartments open to the public at the Oriente, one can also enjoy the plain masculinity of Alfonso XIII's bedroom: brass bed, 'club' furniture, trophies and all.

Philip V's son and successor Ferdinand VI was equally uxorious and melancholic. When his queen, Barbara of Bragança, died in 1758 his habitual depression developed into hopeless melancholy. He shut himself up in the castle of Villaviciosa near Madrid, where he would either prowl about his room like an animal in a cage, or sit motionless for hours on end. He refused to change his clothes or be shaved; he alternated between gorging and starvation. His melancholy turned into madness, with fits of violent rage and attempts to hang himself; so that his death, exactly a year after Barbara's, was a merciful release.

Ferdinand had no children and was followed by his half-brother, Charles III (formerly King of Naples), Elisabeth Farnese's elder son. The lean, stooping, badly-dressed monarch who, in the words of Sir Harold Acton, 'resembled a very distinguished ram' – with his prominent nose, his small, bright, clever eyes, his receding chin and his good-natured expression – was the greatest eighteenth-century king of Spain, and one of the most successful rulers in the whole of Spanish history.

Like most of the other 'enlightened despots', Charles was a munificent patron of architecture and the arts. Most of the great public buildings of Madrid date from his time, notably the Prado gallery. He also completed the new Oriente Palace, begun by his father, and employed Giambattista Tiepolo to decorate it. But though he liked splendid surroundings, he was bored by court ceremonial and is said to have tried to put his court dress on over his hunting-clothes. Hunting and shooting were his greatest passion. They were also the only indulgence in a life that was frugal and austere. His mannish and rather

disagreeable Saxon queen, Maria Amalia, whom he adored, died only a year after his accession to the Spanish throne; for the rest of his life he was faithful to her memory and strictly celibate. To quote Sir Harold Acton again: 'Whenever the slumbering embers of his temperament were stirred, he would jump out of bed and pace his room barefoot until the chill of the night had calmed his fever.'

Charles III's son and successor, Charles IV, resembled his father only in his placid good nature, his passion for field sports and to a certain extent in his looks. He is the king immortalized by the brush of Goya: swarthy, scrawny, gun in hand. Goya also painted his queen, Maria Luisa, who started on her amours even when Charles III was still alive. Soon after her husband came to the throne she took up with her most celebrated lover, Manuel Godoy, who began his career as a private in the Guards; the story went that the queen first set eyes on him when he was on sentry duty at the palace. The easy-going king was content to live in a *ménage-à-trois* in which he was dominated by his wife and she, in turn, by Godoy; Maria Luisa liked to call it 'the Trinity on Earth'.

169 The Oriente, Madrid. The old palace was burnt down in 1734 and this is the new building begun by Philip V in 1738 to the designs of Juan Battista Sacchetti, who had taken over from the deceased Filippo Juvarra as the king's architect. The Oriente was completed by Philip V's son, Charles III, formerly king of the Two Sicilies.

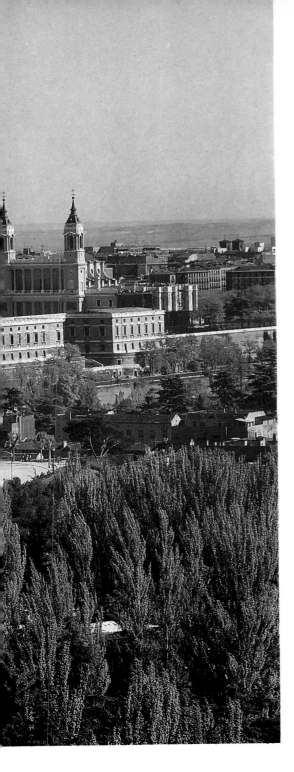

170 (*above right*) Oriente, Madrid: the Hall of Halberdiers. This is where the royal corps of guards used to foregather. The eighteenth-century Santa Barbara tapestries are of the series *History of Joseph, David and Solomon* from drawings by C. Giaquinto and José del Castillo. Some are these artists' original work; others are copied from paintings by Lucas Jordán and Solimena. The children's armour on display includes the equestrian outfit made for Philip IV's son, Prince Belthaser Charles.

After various vicissitudes during the nineteenth and twentieth centuries the Spanish monarchy was restored after a 44-year gap in 1975. The present sovereign, King Juan Carlos, his wife Queen Sofia (a sister of King Constantine) and their family live at the eighteenth-century Zarzuela Palace outside Madrid which used to be a summer retreat of the Spanish court. The name comes from the frothy little operettas, still called *zarzuelas*, which once used to be performed here.

The name of the eccentric Ferdinand VI's refuge, Villaviciosa outside Madrid, should not be confused with the ancestral seat of his Bragançan wife, Vila Viçosa in Portugal. The House of Bragança came to the Portuguese throne in 1640 when the people of Lisbon, tiring of Spanish rule, rose in revolt and offered the crown to the Duke of Bragança, the greatest noble in the kingdom.

In fact the duke had a good hereditary claim to the throne. Paternally he was the illegitimate descendant of João I, the founder of the Aviz line; on his mother's side, he was a great-nephew of the Cardinal-King Henry. He did not, however, have much ambition to be king of Portugal, preferring to live as a country gentleman in his palace at the Vila Viçosa. This favourite palace of the House of Bragança dated from 1501, but was principally of the early seventeenth century when the façade was covered with marble from the quarries near Borba; a third storey was added in the eighteenth century. However, encouraged by his

171 (*above left*) The Zarzuela, near Madrid: the unassuming eighteenth-century residence of the present king and queen of Spain.

172 (*left*) King Juan Carlos and Queen Sofia with their children at home in the Zarzuela Palace.

173 Vila Viçosa, the ancient seat of the House of Bragança.

ambitious and energetic wife, Luisa of Medina-Sidonia, the duke duly accepted and went to Lisbon, where he was crowned as King João IV.

João's son, Afonso VI, was only thirteen when his father died; and he reigned under the Regency of his mother, who vigorously pursued the war with Spain. One of her most successful moves was the marriage of her daughter, Catherine, to the newly-restored Charles II of England, who felt indebted to the House of Bragança since João had sheltered Prince Rupert and the Royalist fleet in 1650. The English sent troops to help Portugal in her fight for freedom, which was finally won in 1668, when the independence of Portugal was formally recognized by Spain. The young king became known as 'Afonso the Victorious', though he made virtually no contribution to the victory, being feeble, vicious and mentally unsound. Indeed, before the war was over, his brother, Dom Pedro, had shut

174 Sintra: the Hall of Swans. The ceiling was decorated with 27 panels each depicting a swan by João of Portugal to commemorate the occasion in 1449 when the ambassadors of Philip the Good, Duke of Burgundy, came to ask for the Infanta's

him up in part of the palace at Vila Viçosa and assumed the Regency. Afonso was later kept in captivity on the island of Terceira in the Azores; then, having tried to murder his gaoler, he was moved to his final prison in the royal palace at Sintra, where he died in 1683.

Sintra is famous for its two vast conical chimneys and has been described as the most Moorish building in the whole of the Iberian peninsula after the Alhambra at Granada. It was not actually built by the Moors but by members of the Aviz dynasty. João (r. 1384–1433) erected the basically Gothic nucleus here in the early fifteenth century and established Sintra as a royal residence. In 1429 he received the ambassadors of Philip the Good, Duke of Burgundy, when they came armed with a pair of swans to ask for his daughter's hand in marriage. João I installed the birds in a tank, while the young Infanta had crown-shaped collars of gold made to put around their elegant necks. When the nuptials duly took place and she left Sintra, her father decorated the ceiling of the room where the creatures had preened themselves with 27 hexagonal panels each depicting a gold-collared swan.

On another famous occasion João I was caught by his English wife, Philippa, John of Gaunt's daughter, osculating with one of her ladies-in-waiting. The king shrewdly followed the example of her grandfather Edward III ('*Honi soit qui mal y pense*'), citing his own motto '*Por Bem*' ('only for good') to the queen. She seemed to take this courtly quip in good part, but the matter was apparently exacerbated by household gossip so João ordered another of his commemorative ceilings. This one was painted with magpies holding in their beaks the Red Rose of Lancaster and a scroll bearing the legend *Por bem*.

The ceiling of the chapel was given a Moorish design and this motif was taken up by Manoel I at the turn of the fifteenth century. It was he who added the distinctive chimneys and introduced the sixty or so different schemes of *azulejo* (ceramics) all over the palace. The Hall of Escutcheons, also added by Manoel I, features the armorial bearings of 72 Portuguese noble families.

The palace at Sintra was considerably enlarged by Pedro's son, João V, one of those splendid, larger-than-life monarchs of the Baroque period. There is indeed a certain resemblance between him and his contemporary, Augustus 'the Strong' of Saxony. João V was passionately devoted to art and his taste was impeccable. In the words of James Lees-Milne, 'his love of God equalled his love of women … he raised a chain of costly churches, and a multitude of natural children'. Fortunately, he was also very rich; wealth was flowing into Portugal at an unprecedented rate from Brazil, following the discovery of the gold of Minas Gerais in 1698. Not having much regard for the native Portuguese styles, João V brought architects, sculptors and painters into Portugal from all over Europe, in order to create his magnificent buildings. The best-known are his vast convent-palace of Mafra – the slightly more cheerful Portuguese counterpart of the Escorial – and the beautiful library at Coimbra University. He also built the town palace of Necessidades in Lisbon (now the Foreign Office) to be near the church which housed the eponymous image of the Virgin Mary from Ericeira.

Mafra is celebrated for the chimes of its bells. Baretti, visiting the convent-palace in 1760, was surprised to hear the bell-ringer playing Handel 'and the

hand in marriage armed with a brace of these
birds. The green-and-white chequer-board
design on the walls around the windows is one
of many types of *azulejo* used in the decoration
of Sintra.

175 Necessidades: the town palace which nowadays houses the Foreign Office.

most difficult lessons of Scarlatti'. William Beckford's nap on the roof in 1787 was rudely interrupted by a sudden 'sonata of chimes'. The chimes were ordered by João V from the bell-founders of Malines; when they queried whether he really wanted to spend so much the extravagant monarch promptly doubled his order.

As early as 1707 João V discussed his plans for Mafra with his architect Frederico Ludovice (formerly Ludwig); work began ten years later on the immensely long façade. The king's apartments lay to the south, the queen's to the north with the church and monastery behind them. Mafra has tended to receive a bad press: 'lacking elegance' (Byron); 'the enchanted palace of a giant' (Beckford); 'a monument to the monotony of royal palaces' (Sir Sacheverell Sitwell). However, its good points include the marbled atrium of the church, the bronze grilles and lamps, the embroidered vestments and, especially, the library, with its Rococo bookcases. The monk who showed Byron the library, with a certain smugness, asked him if the English had any books in their country.

Lord Byron also crops up in the story of Queluz, the loveliest of Portugal's royal palaces which was, strange to relate, designed by a pupil of Ludovice's, Mateus Vicente. The poet featured on a unique pictorial wallpaper here (probably of French manufacture) depicting the Greek Wars of Independence. The figure of Byron was clearly to be seen among the white-kilted Evzones on this paper before it perished when the interior of Queluz was gutted by fire in 1934. Among the happy survivors from this holocaust was a room with *azulejo* wall panels of palm trees and negroes and Chinamen, in blue upon a yellow ground.

This pale pink and pea-green country palace a few miles outside Lisbon was built from 1758 for Dom Pedro (fourth son of João V) who later married his niece, the future Queen Maria. After the double bereavement of losing both her husband and her eldest son, Maria's mind gave way. When William Beckford visited Queluz in 1794, the queen's demented cries of '*Ai Jesus!*' could be heard echoing through the palace; and her surviving son, Dom João, though he was not actually declared Prince Regent until 1799, had already taken the reins of government into his hands. He was so busy that Beckford saw little of him, while making friends with his wife, Dona Carlota Joaquina, who was then not the fierce virago she later became, but a lively young princess who made the 'Caliph of Fonthill' run races with her maids of honour up and down the box alleys.

The gardens at Queluz are its most delightful feature. Laid out by a Frenchman, J. B. Robillon, in terraces, formal parterres and statuary, they complement the irregular contours of the palace. A double staircase leads to the lower garden, with a balustrade and spreading flights of steps. The canal is lined with blue and white tile panels of ships in sail.

The magic of Queluz is nicely captured in William Beckford's *Letters*. He describes the music-making there: the warblings of the Italian *castrati*, the oboe and flute players posted 'at a distance in a thicket of orange and bay trees', and the soft *modinhas* of Brazil that he wished to learn, 'languid, interrupted measures, as if the breath was gone with excess of rapture, and the soul panting to meet the kindred soul . . . with a childish carelessness they steal into the heart'.

The Prince Regent, later João VI (and Emperor of Brazil), conceived a

grandiose scheme for a palace at Ajuda on the hillside behind Belem, but in the event only about a third of it was built. None the less there are some impressive rooms such as the *Sala de Beija-maos* ('Hand-kissing Room'), the marbled *Sale de Marmores* and the *Sala de Tocha*, with its frescoes by Taborda celebrating the glory of João VI. Today the odds and ends of royal memorabilia perhaps provide the main interest at Ajuda: the royal sewing-machine (the first in Portugal), a stuffed bulldog, king-sized commodes, ivory cues in the billiards room.

In 1836 Queen Maria da Glória of Portugal, João VI's granddaughter, married Prince Ferdinand of Saxe-Coburg, a first cousin of Albert (soon to be Prince Consort of Great Britain), whom he resembled in many ways. He was both concerned with bringing Portugal into the nineteenth century and in restoring the great monuments of her past, such as Batalha, the Jerónimos, Mafra, Tomar and the Lisbon Sé. He showed his appreciation of the characteristically Portuguese Manoeline style by using it in the Pena Palace, the castle which he built on the highest peak of the forest-clad mountain at Sintra, 2,000 feet above sea-level, where there had formerly been a convent. The Pena Palace has inevitably been called the 'Portuguese Balmoral'.

Sir Sacheverell Sitwell has written that Pena antedates 'its prototype like an ugly dream'. He describes how

> Knightly figures in armour crop up out of the rocks, an inspiration of the awful Baron Eschwege who was the architect; while in the interior are rooms lined with porcelain, and cement imitating wood. ... The view is splendid from this ugly eyrie.

One could argue that this is a little unfair to what is a spectacular castle of the Romantic Age, a building of which Byron and Beckford (who between them 'discovered' the wild beauties of Sintra) might have approved.

Unlike most of the former royal dynasties, the Portuguese monarchy came to an end even before the First World War. In the carriage museum at the Ajuda Palace a bullet-ridden black landau tells the story. For it was in this coach that King Carlos I, Queen Amelia and their two sons were driving through the Terreiro do Paco in Lisbon in 1908 when assassins opened fire on their carriage, killing the king and the Crown Prince, Dom Luiz Filipe. This murder of the king and his son led to the downfall of the monarchy and to anarchy.

— *Bibliography* —

ACTON, Harold, *The Bourbons of Naples* (1956)
  The Last Bourbons of Naples (1961)
BARTLETT, Vernon, *Northern Italy* (1973)
BENTMANN, Reinhard and LICKES, Heinrich (translated
  by O. Ordish), *Palaces of Europe* (1978)
BIBESCO, Marthe, *Royal Portraits* (1928)
BLUNT, Anthony, *Art and Architecture in France
  1500–1700* (1981)
  Neopolitan Baroque and Rococo Architecture (1975)
BLUNT, Wilfrid, *The Dream King* (1976)
BOYD, Alastair, *The Companion Guide to Madrid and Central
  Spain* (1974)
BRIDGE, Ann and LOWNDES, Susan, *The Selective Traveller
  in Portugal* (1967)
BROOK-SHEPHERD, Gordon, *The Last Habsburg* (1968)
COWLES, Virginia, *The Kaiser* (1963)
CRANKSHAW, Edward, *The Fall of the House of Habsburg*
  (1963)
DUNLOP, Ian, *The Companion Guide to the Ile de France*
  (1979)
FIELD, D. M., *Great Palaces* (1982)
FINESTONE, Jeffrey and MASSIE, Robert K., *The Last
  Courts of Europe* (1981)
FLEETWOOD-HESKETH, Peter, *Guide to the Palace of
  Schönbrunn* (1945)
GUNN, Peter, *The Companion Guide to Southern Italy* (1969)
HAMILTON, G. H., *The Art and Architecture of Russia*
  (1954)
HEMPEL, Eberhard, *Baroque Art and Architecture in
  Central Europe* (1965)
HEYDENREICH, L. W. and LOTZ, W., *Architecture in Italy
  1400–1600* (1974)
HOWARD, Philip, *The Royal Palaces* (1970)
JUDD, Denis, *Eclipse of Kings* (1976)
JORDAN, Ruth, *Sophie Dorothea* (1971)
KAVLI, Guthorm, *Norwegian Architecture* (1958)
KENNETT, Audrey, *Palaces of Leningrad* (1973)
KROLL, Maria and LINDSEY, Jason, *Europe's Royal
  Families* (1979)
KUBLER, G., and SORIA, M., *Art and Architecture in Spain
  and Portugal and Their American Dominions 1500–1800*
  (1959)

LEES-MILNE, James, *Baroque in Italy* (1959)
  Baroque in Spain and Portugal (1960)
  (introduction), *Buildings of Europe, Volume I:
  Renaissance; Volume II: Baroque* (1962)
  William Beckford (1976)
LONGFORD, Elizabeth, *Victoria R.I.* (1964)
LUKE, Sir Harry, *In the Margin of History* (1933)
MACLEAN, Fitzroy, *Holy Russia* (1978)
MASSIE, Robert K., *Nicholas and Alexandra* (1968)
MASSON, Georgina, *The Companion Guide to Rome* (1965)
  Italian Villas and Palaces (1966)
MITFORD, Nancy, *Frederick the Great* (1970)
  The Sun King (1966)
MONTAGUE-SMITH, Patrick and MONTGOMERY-
  MASSINGBERD, Hugh, *Royal Palaces, Castles & Homes*
  (1981)
MONTGOMERY-MASSINGBERD, Hugh (ed.), *Burke's Guide to
  The Royal Family* (1973)
  *Burke's Royal Families of the World, Volume I: Europe
  & Latin America* (1977)
MYHILL, Henry, *Portugal* (1972)
PAGET, Walburga, *Embassies of Other Days* (1923)
PALMER, Alan, *Frederick the Great* (1974)
  The Kaiser (1978)
PEVSNER, Sir Nikolaus, *A History of Building Types* (1976)
RASCHAUER, Oskar, *Schönbrunn* (1960)
RICHARDS, J. M., *Who's Who in Architecture* (1977)
ROBINSON, John Martin, *Royal Residences* (1982)
ROSENBERG, J., SLIVE, S., and TER KUILE, E. H., *Dutch
  Art and Architecture 1600–1800* (1966)
SEWARD, Desmond, *The Bourbon Kings of France* (1976)
SINCLAIR, Andrew, *The Other Victoria* (1982)
SITWELL, Sacheverell (introduction), *Great Palaces* (1964)
  Portugal and Madeira (1954)
  Southern Baroque Art (1924)
  Southern Baroque Revisited (1968)
  Spain (1975)
SKOVGAARD, J. A., *A King's Architecture* (1973)
TUCHMAN, Barbara, *The Proud Tower* (1966)
WHITTLE, Tyler, *Victoria and Albert at Home* (1980)
WINDSOR, Duke of, *A King's Story* (1951)
YARWOOD, Doreen, *The Architecture of Europe* (1974)

Acknowledgements

The author wishes to thank Felicity Mortimer who first invited him to write this book on behalf of Burke's Peerage publications in 1979; and Elisabeth Ingles, Laurence King and Susan Bolsom-Morris of John Calmann and Cooper, who have made it a reality. Gillon Aitken, Evelyn Archdale, Juan Balansó, Anna Barlow, Lydia Bierbrier, Christine Comonte, Prince George Galitzine, Mary Killen, Caroline Montgomery-Massingberd, Michael Sayer, Hugo Vickers, David Williamson and Carole Winlaw have all rendered useful advice and practical assistance. The author's chief debts of gratitude are to Mark Bence-Jones, whose historical mastery has been of the utmost value throughout, and to Judy Airy, researcher *sans pareil*.

The author and John Calmann and Cooper Ltd would like to thank those who have kindly provided photographs. Sources are listed below.

Reproduced by Gracious Permission of Her Majesty The Queen: 99, 100, 101, 103, 104, 105, 106
Actualit, Brussels: 123, 124
Aerofilms Ltd, Boreham Wood: 5, 95, 135
Alinari, Florence: 83, 141, 144, 145, 146, 148
J. Allan Cash, London: 50, 72, 107, 125, 133, 134, 138
Anderson, Florence: 147, 153
Wayne Andrews, Grosse Pointe, Michigan: 139, 157
Austrian National Tourist Office, Vienna: 37, 53
Abilio Barata & Mario Soares, Lisbon: 173, 174, 175, 176
Barnaby's Picture Library, London: 40, 127
Bavaria Verlag, Munich: 25, 35, 38, 42, 77, 132, 163
Bayerische Verwaltung der staatlichen Schlösser, Gärten und Seen, Munich: 75
Belgian National Tourist Office, Brussels: 120, 121
John Bethell, St Albans: 88
Bulloz, Paris: 15
Camera Press, London: 52, 137, 171
Crown copyright. Reproduced by permission of the Comptroller of Her Majesty's Stationery Office, London: 90, 92, 94, 97, 98
Dalde Fotografo, Madrid: 172
Edimedia, Paris: 16, 18, 23, 24
Prince George Galitzine, London: 36
Giraudon, Paris: 3, 4, 7
Michael Holford, Loughton, Essex: 2, 8, 9, 10, 11, 13, 17, 93, 159, 166
Angelo Hornak, London: 66, 78, 80, 81
John Jedbo, Copenhagen: 130

Victor Kennet/Robert Harding Picture Library, London: 27, 28, 29, 32, 34
A. F. Kersting, London: 21, 43, 45, 54, 57, 64, 65, 68, 86, 89, 91, 96, 128
Dalibor Kusák/Dilia, Prague: 49
Luxembourg Tourist Office: 114
Mansell Collection, London: 12, 102, 109, 129
Bildarchiv Foto Marburg: 39, 44, 47, 48, 56, 58, 59, 60, 62, 82, 84
MAS, Barcelona: 162, 167
Netherlands Information Service, The Hague: 115, 116, 117, 118, 119, 122
Werner Neumeister, Munich/Bayerische Verwaltung der staatlichen Schlösser, Gärten und Seen, Munich: 70, 73, 74, 79
Novosti Press Agency, London: 26, 30, 31, 33
Oronoz, Madrid: 164
Van Phillips, London: 22
Popperfoto, London: 108, 110, 111, 112, 113
Réunion des Musées Nationaux, Paris: 19
Royal Collections, Stockholm: 131
Salmer, Barcelona: 158, 160, 161, 168, 169, 170
Scala, Florence: 1, 6, 14, 41, 150, 151, 154, 155, 156
Helga Schmidt-Glassner, Stuttgart: 55, 67, 69, 71, 85, 87
Edwin Smith, Saffron Walden: 61, 140, 142, 143, 149, 165
Tetrel/Explorer/Vision International, London: 76
John Topham Picture Library, Edenbridge: 20
Ullstein Bilderdienst, Berlin: 51, 63
Zefa Picture Library (UK) Ltd, London: 46, 126, 136

Index